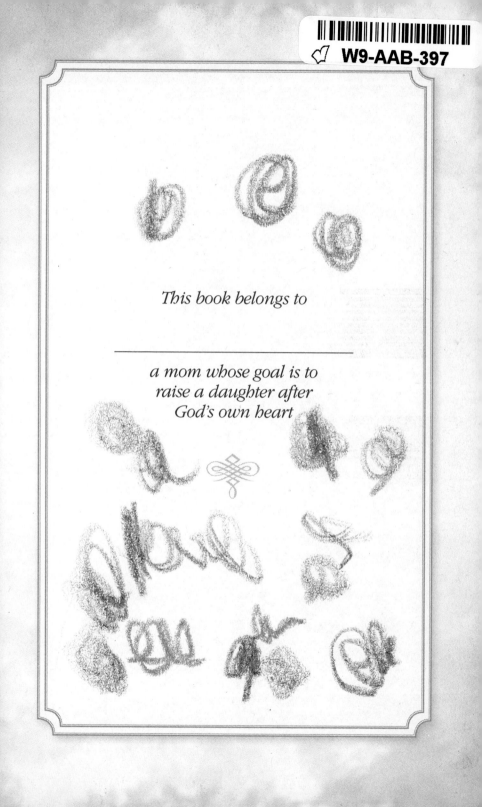

This book belongs to

_____

*a mom whose goal is to
raise a daughter after
God's own heart*

Raising a Daughter After God's Own Heart

Elizabeth George

HARVEST HOUSE PUBLISHERS

EUGENE, OREGON

Cover by Garborg Design Works, Savage, Minnesota

Cover photo © Corbis / Inmagine

RAISING A DAUGHTER AFTER GOD'S OWN HEART
Copyright © 2011 by Elizabeth George
Published by Harvest House Publishers
Eugene, Oregon 97402
www.harvesthousepublishers.com

Library of Congress Cataloging-in-Publication Data
  George, Elizabeth, 1944-
  Raising a daughter after God's own heart / Elizabeth George.
     p. cm.
  ISBN 978-0-7369-1772-8 (pbk.)
  ISBN 978-0-7369-4158-7 (eBook)
  1. Mothers and daughters—Religious aspects—Christianity. 2. Parenting—Religious aspects—Christianity. 3. Mothers—Religious life. I. Title.
  BV4529.18.G47 2011
  248.8'431—dc23

                                                           2011017122

Printed in the United States of America

        12 13 14 15 16 17 18 19 / BP-SK / 10 9 8 7 6 5 4 3 2

This book is lovingly dedicated to
my cherished daughters after God's own heart—
Katherine and Courtney
and my treasured granddaughters
after God's own heart—
Taylor, Katie, Grace, and Lilyanna

"May our daughters be like graceful pillars,
carved to beautify a palace"

(PSALM 144:12 NLT).

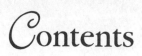

Contents

Mom to Mom

For decades my husband and I have prayed about passing on our faith in Christ to our daughters and then one day, Lord willing, seeing our girls pass on their love for Jesus to their children. Well, I can't tell you how excited Jim was one day several weeks ago. He couldn't wait to get home and tell me what had happened. He had taken our little six-year-old granddaughter, Grace, to her ballet lesson, something Jim had never done before. It all came about because our daughter was busy, and Jim volunteered to help her by doing ballet taxi duty. And on this day, God chose to bless Jim in a special way. Here's what happened.

On the Saturday this all took place, attendance at the ballet school was mandatory because the students were preparing for their year-end recital. Grace *loves* to go to her lessons. She's lean, graceful, light on her feet, and excels as a perfect little ballerina. But on this required rehearsal day, Grace's entire family was involved in a seminar at their church.

Now Courtney, our daughter and Grace's mom, was helping with a children's program at church while the adults were involved in the seminar. And Grace wanted to be at the church and participate in the children's program too. The solution? Jim would pick Gracie up for the one-hour lesson, then immediately whisk her back to the church.

Well, all was going well until Jim arrived at the church to take Grace to the rehearsal. When he pulled up at the curb, he spotted her and her mom coming out of the children's classroom, and Grace was crying her little heart out. Jim blurted out,

"What happened? Is everything okay? Is she hurt? Sick?" Her mom explained, "Grace was enjoying the children's Bible group so much she didn't want to leave."

Needless to say, Jim and Courtney both worked overtime convincing little Grace that she would soon be back at church and spend the rest of the day with the other kids until the seminar was over. Finally, with these assurances, Grace wiped away her tears and went off to her lesson.

After the ballet practice session, when Jim was driving her back to the church, little Gracie, who had been learning how to read, piped up from the backseat and said, "You know what I want for my birthday?" (She said this when her birthday was still six months away!) Before Jim could respond, Grace announced, "Now that I can read, I want a real Bible so I can read it as much as I want!"

This is a sweet story, isn't it? Every mom-in-Christ yearns for her children to love Jesus and cherish God's Word—that they would follow after God's own heart. I know this doesn't always happen, but as one of God's moms, you are asked by Him to do your best, to do your part, and then leave the outcome to Him.

That's what this book is all about. Doing your best. Doing your part. Living out your God-assigned roles—or missions—as a mom who desires to raise a daughter who loves the Lord. I can't guarantee your results—whatever happens is up to God. But what I *can* offer are personal experiences, wisdom gleaned from God's Word, advice from other moms, practical suggestions to get you going, and tons of encouragement!

This book won't answer all your questions. And it won't provide all the answers. But it will give you one more resource for your parenting. It will give you one more opportunity to roll up your mothering sleeves and apply God's Word and His principles to your efforts to raise a daughter after God's own heart. And no, attaining this goal won't be easy—a prize this grand is never easily achieved. But the rewards of passing on the truths about God to your daughter and watching her grow into a woman after God's own heart will be great—and the fruit will last for all eternity. God promises, "The LORD is good; His mercy is everlasting, and His truth endures to all generations" (Psalm 100:5).

Chapter 1

The Bell Sheep

Part 1—Earning Your Bell

You shall love the LORD your God with all your heart,
with all your soul, and with all your strength.
And these words which I command you today
shall be in your heart.

—DEUTERONOMY 6:5

On a recent Christmas Sunday, my husband, Jim, and I and our family of 14 arrived at a church service extra early to make sure we didn't end up in the "Standing Room Only" section for this special occasion. With my bulletin in hand and several minutes to spare before the service started, I opened my Bible and looked up the Scripture passage the pastor would focus on during his message. Then I read through some additional teaching notes and commentary in the margin of my Bible. One article was entitled "The Bell Sheep."

The bell sheep? What in the world is that? I wondered. I read on. The article explained that when a shepherd noticed a sheep who willingly followed him and stayed near him, he hung a bell around the neck of that sheep so the flock would follow the bell sheep...who, in turn, was following the shepherd.[1]

Knowing I would begin writing *Raising a Daughter After God's Own Heart* as soon as the Christmas holiday was over, I almost jumped out of my seat when I read this. I was shouting out in my mind, "That's it! That's it! A *mom* should be the bell sheep for her daughter!"

And it's true! When we as mothers stay close to Jesus—as close as close can be, and when we love Him with all our heart just the way Jesus said to, and when we willingly follow Him and His Word, guess what? We become His bell sheep for our daughters to follow. Our girls observe—and copy—our behavior. They can—and will—follow our example. We become their very own personal walking, living, real flesh and blood, visual example of what it means to be a child, girl, tween, teen, and woman after God's own heart.

How to Be a Bell Sheep...in Three Verses

Finally Christmas was over, meaning it was D-Day for me—or more accurately, W-Day as in Writing Day. So I sat down to begin and wondered and prayed, "Where does Christian childrearing really begin? And what is Thing 1, Goal 1 for a mom?"

In a few seconds I had the answer! And it came from God's Word. It was packaged in three verses I had discovered as a young mom, and also as a baby Christian. I flashed back on those early new-believer days of excitement, of newness, of need as I hungered to find out for the first time what God teaches about...everything! And especially "What in the world am I supposed to do with two little toddling girls?"

I'm so glad a wise woman had advised me to read in my new Bible every day. Well, the day arrived when I made it to the book of Deuteronomy. And there I hit gold when my eyes landed on Deuteronomy 6:5-7. I was stunned. Amazed. Thrilled! God was actually showing me *His* guidelines for raising my own little daughters, then only one-and-a-half and two-and-a-half years old. And in only three verses! How practical is that? Here's what I read over and over again and finally memorized:

> You shall love the LORD your God with all your heart, with all your soul, and with all your strength. And these words which I command you today shall be in your heart. You shall teach them diligently to your

children, and shall talk of them when you sit in your house, when you walk by the way, when you lie down, and when you rise up.

I adore these verses because they are packed with clear communication to moms. God goes straight to the heart of the matter—the parent's heart, the *mom's* heart. He knows we become what we love. So He is utterly straightforward about where we are to place our love: We are to love Him supremely.

Two Questions to Ask Yourself

Believe me, I thought through this powerful passage—a lot! Then I took it apart word by word and thought by thought. And I came up with two questions I constantly asked my heart during those days with little girls, and still ask even today with two married daughters who are now raising their daughters. (After all, a mom is always a mom!)

Heart Question #1: What—and whom—do I love?

We "love" a lot of things for a lot of different reasons. But God prescribes perimeters and scope for our love. He tells us what *not* to love: "Do not love the world or the things in the world" (1 John 2:15). And He tells us what we *are* to love and where our love is to be focused—we are to "love the Lord" (Deuteronomy 6:5).

But hold on. The Lord goes a step further and demands *all* of our love. He wants us to love *Him* with every fiber of our being—every breath, every ounce of energy, every thought, every emotion and passion, every choice. He wants us to love Him. He wants us to think first of Him and to desire above all else to please Him. And He wants that love to be intense and total, "with all your heart, with all your soul, and with all your strength." As writer Matthew Henry summarizes, "He that is our all demands our all."[2]

Matthew Henry continues on to point out that our love for God is to be a strong one that is lived out with great enthusiasm and fervency of affection. It is to be a love that burns like a sacred fire, a love that causes our every affection to flow toward Him.

Now, apply this information about the strength of this kind of love for God and think about the love you have for your daughter, for your children. I'm sure you've heard others say, "There is no love like a mother's love." And it's true! From the split second we know a baby is on the way, all our thoughts, dreams, prayers, and goals are channeled toward that little one. We are completely consumed and preoccupied by this tiny being. As the baby grows within us, our love blossoms and our commitment to it grows right along with our expanding body.

Immediately we begin to prepare physically for his or her arrival by meticulously taking care of our health. Healthy mom equals healthy baby, we're told. We also prepare physically by setting up a nursery area for the new little addition. A bassinet or crib. A blanket. A mobile. Clothes. Supplies. Loads of diapers! Sometimes we even paint or remodel a room.

The more you love the Lord, the better you shall love your earthly dearest daughter.

Then we moms get to work preparing our schedule. Maybe we have to quit a job or arrange for a leave of absence. Oh, and we have to find a pediatrician, as well as make time for our own doctor appointments. And, if we're smart, we begin to prepare by gathering wisdom and information from our own moms, other moms, and from classes, books, and the Internet.

But as much as we obsess and focus on an approaching child, God wants us to obsess and focus even more on Him. That's because the more we love Him, the more we will know about love. And the more we know about love, the more we will know about how to love. And the more we know about how to love, the more we will love our baby, our child, our daughter. I like what C.S. Lewis wrote about his love for God and how it affected his relationship with his wife: "When I have learnt to love God better than my earthly dearest, I shall love my earthly dearest better than I do now."[3] Mom, your love for God will prepare you to love your child. The more you love the Lord, the better you shall love your earthly dearest daughter.

So...God's first assignment to any and every mother is to love

Him above all else. If you are a sold-out, on-fire, hot-hearted, committed-to-God woman, you will be infinitely further down the road to being the kind of mom who, by His grace, can raise a daughter after God's own heart. Because all your love centers upon God, and because you follow Him with all your heart, you will qualify to lead your daughter to follow God too—to be…well…God's bell sheep for her.

Heart Question #2: What's in my heart?

I don't know what's in your heart, and I'm working on what's in mine! But God tells both of us what is supposed to be there, what He wants to be there. Here it is: He says, "These words which I command you today shall be in your heart" (verse 6).

And here's the scene surrounding these words: In Deuteronomy 6, Moses is in the final weeks of his life. It has been 40 years since God's people left Egypt, 40 years of homeless wanderings in the desert. At last a new generation was poised to enter into the Promised Land. But before they move out, Moses restates the Law one more time to this new generation that had been born in the wilderness. Because this next generation had married and now had—and would have—children, he addresses their spiritual responsibility as parents. As Moses speaks, he doesn't want these moms and dads to merely *hear* the words of the Law and the Ten Commandments. No, he wants more, way more! He wants the words of the Law to go beyond their ears and reside *in their hearts*.

You may want to look again at Deuteronomy 6:6, but it tells us that God's Word, the Bible, is to be *in* our hearts. Other passages in the Bible send us this same message:

> This Book of the Law shall not depart from your mouth, but you shall meditate in it day and night (Joshua 1:8).
>
> Your word I have hidden in my heart, that I might not sin against you (Psalm 119:11).
>
> My son, keep my words, and treasure my commands within you…bind them on your fingers; write them on the tablet of your heart (Proverbs 7:1,3).

Let the word of Christ dwell in you richly (Colossians 3:16).

The message is repeated...and loud, isn't it? And clear! God's Word is to be *in* our heart. He asks this of you and me as moms. Why? Because when truth resides in your heart, then you have something to pass on to your daughter. She benefits! And you benefit too: As a mother you have something to guide you when you need help, strength, wisdom, and perseverance in your role as a mom, as a bell sheep. Don't get me wrong—having and raising a child is perhaps the greatest earthly blessing you will ever enjoy. But, at the same time, it is the greatest challenge. But take heart, mom! God's Word will always be there in you, with you, and for you as you guide your daughter in the ways of the Lord.

So...God's second assignment for you as a mom is to be committed to His Word. You are to do whatever it takes to embed the teachings of the Bible in your heart, soul, and mind. As the saying goes, "You cannot impart what you do not possess." The same is true of moms. To teach and guide, lead and raise a daughter after God's own heart presupposes and requires that God's truth be in your heart first. *Then* you possess something to impart. *Then* you have the most important thing to pass on to your precious daughter—the truth about God and the grace He extends through His Son, Jesus.

Becoming the Bell Sheep

I hope your heart is responding fervently to our initial glimpse at this primary role in the life of a mom after God's own heart—that of being your daughter's very own bell sheep. But maybe you are feeling like you need a little help. Well, read on to find out *how* to become the bell sheep. Practical help is on the way!

Chapter 1

The Bell Sheep

Part 2—Ringing Your Bell

You shall teach them diligently to your children,
and shall talk of them when you sit in your house,
when you walk by the way, when you lie down,
and when you rise up.

—DEUTERONOMY 6:6-7

When my girls were young, I didn't know about the bell sheep. But if I had, I would have wanted with all my heart to be one. And I would have been praying, "Oh, dear Father! You know how much I desire to be a bell sheep for my daughters. My greatest goal in life is to lead them to Jesus and teach them His ways." I'm imagining this same heart-cry is being lifted heavenward from your soul's core too.

As you've probably learned, *knowing* there is something God wants you to do is crucial. And *wanting* to do what God wants you to do is vital. But if you don't know *how* to do what it is God wants you to do, you can become extremely frustrated.

So now we come to the big issue of *how* do I do this thing God wants—and expects—me to do? Well, here we go!

Yes, but How?

How does a mom help her daughter develop a heart for God? Deuteronomy 6:7 comes to the rescue and answers this question for you and me. God says, "You shall teach them diligently to your children" (verse 7). A mom who wholeheartedly loves the Lord and holds God's words in her heart is to *teach* them to her sons and daughters.

"To teach"—There are two key ways to teach—by model and by mouth. And there are some basic practices you can follow for teaching effectively. I have a degree in education and have taught preschoolers, students from grades seven through twelve, and adults taking night school classes. Teaching was a job and I took it seriously. I developed my lesson plans for each day, week, month, semester, and school year. And I studied and prepared in advance for each day's classes.

I also have a daughter who homeschools. I am in constant awe of her commitment. She plans out each year. She searches for materials for five children and their respective grade levels. She orders curriculum to arrive well before back-to-school day so she can preview it. Then she plans in advance the best way to teach, lead, and guide the five of them through each day of study.

Now picture this: I taught subjects that had nothing to do with God or with being a Christian, and so does my daughter. Imagine the effort we both put into teaching information and facts. And here in Deuteronomy 6:7, God is telling both of us—and all moms—to teach our children His Word, His ways, His truth. Now, *this* is life-changing stuff! The Bible is wisdom that will guide their lives and their choices. It is truth that will pierce a heart and bring a daughter to Christ. So be aware that every time you teach God's Word you, the bell sheep, are ringing your bell! You are signaling to your daughter the priceless value of the treasure of the Scriptures.

This is exactly what happened in the New Testament to Timothy. As the apostle Paul said of Timothy, his trusted associate in ministry, "from childhood you have known the Holy Scriptures, which are able to make you wise for salvation through faith which is in Christ Jesus" (2 Timothy 3:15). God's Word is dynamite! And Timothy's mom and grandmom, a mother/daughter tag team after God's own heart, were faithful to ring their bells! They were faithful to teach him the sacred truths of the Bible, which paved the way for Timothy's salvation. Mom and grandmom did their part—they fulfilled their mission to teach God's saving truth. And God certainly did His part!

Time out for a second. I'm thinking as we pause here, shouldn't a mom after God's own heart who wants to raise a daughter after God's own heart take her teaching of Scripture seriously? If you are in this position, shouldn't you be committed to...

> ...instructing your daughter in God's ways?
>
> ...planning to some extent how you will accomplish this goal?
>
> ...scheduling a time each day for some kind of formal Bible time with her?
>
> ...encouraging her to have some time alone with God, a quiet time?
>
> ...coaching her in ways to have daily devotions?
>
> ...searching for age-appropriate materials and talking with other moms about how they teach their children biblical truth?
>
> ...praying daily about this mission from God, this teacher role He has personally given you?

"To teach diligently"—Next God tells us in verse 7 to "teach them diligently to your children." The "them" is *what* you are to teach—God's Word and His commands. And "diligently" is *how* you are to teach—being purposeful and conscientious in a task or duty.

Think about this for a minute: What are you diligent about? Some women diligently floss their teeth. Others are so diligent they would never miss their daily exercise or walk, or be late to work, or fail to pay a bill on time. I know women who are so serious about every bite of food they put into their mouths that they diligently record what they eat in a daily log. On and on goes the list of life instances in which women choose to be diligent instead of careless, or lazy, or negligent.

Now switch your thoughts to doing what God says, to being diligent to teach spiritual truth to your daughter...versus leaving this all-important assignment to someone else, such as a church leader or a Christian school or a grandparent. Don't get me wrong! These are wonderful and needed resources. But they are to be your partners in imparting truth, not your substitutes. You as a mother are to be the bell sheep who rings the bell of truth like crazy! You, mom, are to be the primary model and teacher of truth to your daughter.

Well, thank the Lord He doesn't leave moms on their own. This isn't mission impossible. No, it's mission possible. God knows most moms don't have a degree in education or training in teaching. And, whew, God doesn't expect this or demand it! Aren't you glad? Instead, He tells us how to teach and what this teaching involves. He says, "You...shall talk of them when you sit in your house, when you walk by the way, when you lie down, and when you rise up" (verse 7).

No matter who you are, or what you do or don't know about teaching—or how busy you are!—God expects *you* to pour God's Word out of your heart and into your daughter's heart. All you have to do is:

Step 1, love the Lord with all your heart;

Step 2, have God's Word in your heart; and now

Step 3, teach His truths diligently.

By...what? Talking?! You mean that's all? That's it? Yes, that's it—by talking.

Now I ask you, you're a woman. How hard can talking be? Why, we girls are the world's experts when it comes to talking!

And note *where* all our mother-to-daughter talking and teaching is to take place—*at home*. Nothing could be easier or more natural or more convenient than home sweet home! You don't need elaborate plans. You don't need to dress up or go anywhere. You don't need to start the car. And you don't need to spend any money. No. God simply says that "when you sit in your house," you are to talk about Him.

Whew again—this one's easy! You sit to relax. You sit to eat.

You sit to visit. You sit to read. You sit to work on a craft together. And you sit whenever you're in the car together. No matter what your daughter's age is, these natural, low-key, sitting instances provide prime opportunities to talk about the Lord and His love and His promises...and His Son.

And "when you *walk by the way*" you are to talk about the Lord. From babyhood, to toddler times, to little girl, to schoolgirl, you'll be walking with your daughter. That's your special time for talking about the Lord. So...

Got a newborn? You will walk...and walk...and walk each time you calm your crying, ill, or restless baby. And you'll put in miles pushing her stroller. And you'll find yourself talking baby talk to her. I laughed out loud when I read this true-to-motherhood quip: "Being a mom means talking to your baby all the time."[4] So go ahead and talk all you want. It will develop the habit in you—and tune your baby girl's heart to your voice.

How about a school-age daughter? If you walk your young daughter to school or to and from the school bus stop, you get to talk about the Lord. Tell her how He will help her through her time at school, with her test or report, with making friends. If you walk to the mailbox down the road, take your daughter along and chat about the wonders of the Lord and what it means to know Him. Let her know how she can trust Him and talk to Him anytime, anywhere, and ask for His help. When you walk together through the grocery store or the mall, again, make that an opportunity to talk about God and His provision and blessings. If there's a breathtaking sunrise, sunset, rainbow, or wonder of nature—a bird's nest, blooming flowers, even something as small as a dandelion, go outside and marvel at God's handiwork together. And while you're at it, do as the psalmist did and "talk" of His doings. "Praise" the Lord for His mighty acts and His greatness. "Declare" His faithfulness.[5]

And then come the teen years. Hopefully you and your daughter have developed the habit of talking to each other about any and every thing, and especially about the Lord. So during her teen years, when things can get a little weird, and she may even see you as a little weird, you can still talk because of your history of talking. Believe me, if you are available, and care, and give her your love and attention, she will spill all!

And if you haven't developed this early habit of talking, don't worry and don't give up. Just be sure you start now. Start talking, even if your daughter doesn't seem to be listening. She *is* hearing, and what you say in loving wisdom *will* be filed away in her mind and heart. And it won't go away. She won't be able to shake it or forget it. Draw your strength from the Lord and speak the truth in love (Ephesians 4:15). And if your daughter won't talk to you,

Home is the natural 24/7, morning-to-evening place to impress truth upon your daughter.

that's okay. Just know before God that you talked, just like He asked you to do. You faithfully rang your bell. You shared truth from His Word. And take comfort in the fact that God promises His Word will *not* go forth in vain but *will* accomplish His purposes (Isaiah 55:11).

And to end each day and start the next, God tells you what to do in Deuteronomy 6:7: "When you lie down, and when you rise up," talk! *Talk* about the Lord, and keep on talking about Him. You can help even your tiny young daughter start her days and end them with thoughts of God in her mind. You can greet your waking girl with, "This is the day the LORD has made; we will rejoice and be glad in it" (Psalm 118:24). Or you can call out, "There you are, my precious blessing from the Lord! Good morning!" And at night, prayer is the perfect way to put a little—and big!—girl to bed. It puts her day and all that happened to rest. It calms all sorrows and soothes every hurt from the day. And it quells her fears. Like David testified, "I lay down and slept; I awoke, for the LORD sustained me," and "I will both lie down in peace and sleep; for You alone, O LORD, make me dwell in safety" (Psalm 3:5 and 4:8).

So...another of God's assignments to any and every mom is to constantly be teaching and talking to your daughter about the Lord you love. Teaching and talking. And talking and teaching. Or put another way, ringing your bell! I hope you are grasping that being a Christian mom is more than taking your children to church. Home is a sort of church too. Home is the natural 24/7, morning-to-evening place to impress truth upon your daughter. Home is where she gets to see and hear every day how important the Lord is to you. Wherever and whenever the two of you are together is God's opportunity for you to tell her about Him. So take advantage of the gift of such times. And if they are too few and far between, make it happen. Create the times together. In his book *Shepherding a Child's Heart*, author Tedd Tripp gives this challenge to parents:

> You shepherd your child in God's behalf. The task God has given you is not one that can be conveniently scheduled. It is a pervasive task. Training and shepherding are going on whenever you are with your children. Whether waking, walking, talking or resting, you must be involved in helping your child to understand life, himself and his needs from a biblical perspective.[6]

But What If…

I realize this ideal scenario does not happen in every mother/daughter relationship. Maybe the family you grew up in was not a Christian family. God knows that. He knows all about it—all about what you missed, and all about what you know and don't know about being a Christian family and mom. So know that your mission is to *begin where you are* to follow the Lord. It's never too late to receive Christ as Savior, to begin loving the Lord and growing in grace and in the knowledge of Him and His Word. You can choose any day—today, if you haven't already—to begin diligently teaching the daughter you love, and talking to her about the God you love and who loves her. Point her to God. Encourage her in the Lord. Teach her what you know about Him from experience and from study. Pray for her with your every heartbeat. See her spiritual growth into a daughter after God's own heart as your calling, your mission assignment from God. Commit to doing your part, and trust God to do His.

Perhaps you are thinking, *This woman is crazy!* Well, I wouldn't blame you. But I will tell you I am crazy about God, crazy about my two daughters, and crazy about my four granddaughters. I will also tell you that I am passionate and passionately sold out to my role as a woman, mom, and grandmom after God's own heart. It's just so clear what God wants His moms to be and do. Your daughter has no other mother. *You* are the one He has chosen to teach her. And if you don't, what if no one does?

Here's a powerful description of what an all-out, all-or-nothing love for God and our daughters looks like. Let it encourage you today and in the decades of mothering to come:

> ...my mission is clear. I cannot be bought, compromised, detoured, lured away, turned back, diluted, or delayed. I will not flinch in the face of sacrifice, hesitate in the presence of adversity...I won't give up, shut up, let up, or slow up.[7]

You Can Do It!

Each of the following suggestions is something you can do to contribute toward becoming the mom you dream of being. And each one betters your life...and your daughter's too. Here we go:

Analyze your day.

Think through the rhythm of your day and pinpoint your discretionary time, the time when you have a choice about how it is used, when you can choose how it's spent. There is always time to do what's important to you. You'll need to find the time to get to know God—to put first things first.

Design a quiet time.

Once you've carved out a special time to be with God, begin reading your Bible—even for just ten minutes. It's been calculated that if you simply read your Bible for ten minutes a day, you will read through all of it in one year. That's a doable task for you as a bell sheep whose life goal is leading your daughter to Jesus. There are scores of activities that fill your day. So steal ten minutes from a nonimportant activity like time on the Internet, time talking on the phone, time watching TV. Make a daily appointment with God and allow Him to speak to your heart from His Word.

Memorize Scripture.

Here's a statistic for you: People remember about 40 percent of what they read. Wouldn't it be nice to remember 100 percent? Well, you can if you memorize verses from the Bible. That's what someone told me as a new Christian, and I followed their advice. As I shared earlier, as soon as I read Deuteronomy 6:5-7, I learned it by heart. I also picked out some verses that would help me with my daily life, including the daily challenge of being a mom after God's own heart. Like "I can do all things [including be a mom!] through Christ who strengthens me" (Philippians 4:13). Once you store up some verses in your heart, you'll find that wherever you are and whatever is happening, you can remember God's words to you. And just think—as a bell sheep, you can draw your daughter to Jesus as you speak His words to her.

Read about parenting.

In my mentoring ministry, one of my assignments for the women I meet with and give my time to is that they read five minutes a day on a variety of topics. They can pick the topics and the books. They can buy them, borrow them, or check them out of the church library. I do this because I've been reading on my own topics for five minutes a day for decades! For instance, I've been reading five minutes a day on marriage and family for what seems like forever. The same goes for time and life management. And health.

If you do this too, you will amaze yourself as you become an expert on your subjects by merely reading five minutes a day on them. You will also be super motivated because the topic and your new knowledge is fresh in your mind. Instead of dreading something, you'll look forward to approaching it differently and trying some new techniques or methods. Your reading will serve as a reminder and an instructor to pay attention to the areas of your life you targeted for growth. Pray, and then choose your subjects. Just be sure as a mom that childrearing is one of them.

Write a letter to God about your daughter.

Then read the letter to Him as a prayer. Prayer involves God. So now there are two of you taking on the challenge of raising a daughter after God's own heart. It will seal your commitment to becoming God's kind of mom so, Lord willing and by His grace, your daughter grows to be God's kind of girl. File your "My Prayer to Be a Mom After God's Own Heart" away where it is handy and can be prayed often, even daily. Your prayer is another good reminder each day to keep on keeping on in your goals as a mom and your goals for your daughter. And here's an idea: Each year on your daughter's birthday, slip a copy of your prayer into her birthday card. Be sure to tell her where you were and what you were feeling when you wrote it. What a gift!

Mom's Think Pad

Before you move on to your next Mom Mission, take a minute or two to think about what you can do to track with God as a mom. Make some plans of your own to take a few small steps that make a big difference.

1. I'm awfully busy, but I want to be the mom God wants me to be! What are several things I can do—or not do—to create some time to get into God's Word? I want to be a mom after God's own heart!

2. I want to set a goal to memorize Deuteronomy 6:5-7. Here's my checklist:

   Write these verses on an index card and carry it with me.

   Pick a daily five-minute time slot that works for my schedule, during which I can memorize these verses.

   Write out each verse ten times.

   Copy these verses on several more index cards and post them on the refrigerator door, bathroom mirror, computer, car dashboard.

   Ask my daughter to help me memorize these verses, to listen to me recite them, to be my audience, my checker, my best helper!

3. What are some ways I can "teach" my daughter about God and His Word by "talking" about Him...

   ...when we are sitting together?

   ...when we are walking together?

   ...when she is going to bed or going down for her nap?

   ...when she gets up?

4. What are some ways I can be more faithful and "diligent" in passing on God's truth to my daughter?

5. Do I need to be mentored in my own spiritual growth? Who could help me? Or is there a class I can take? A group I can join? A book I can read?

The Prayer Warrior

Part 1—Remembering to Pray

Until now you have asked nothing in My name.
Ask, and you will receive, that your joy may be full.
—JOHN 16:24

*H*ere's a true confession: It took me five years to finally agree to write this book about raising daughters to follow God. Each time I even thought about it, I cowered.

Well, if you are reading this, you know I obviously took the plunge. Even after I said yes and began praying daily about how to approach writing this book about raising daughters, I have to admit I had some doubts and hesitations—lots of them! Like all moms, I questioned my own experience as a parent with two children—two daughters. Raising children is never done perfectly, but it is usually done with a heart of unmeasurable love...and hope.

Perhaps the most encouraging wisdom and insight I received as a young, wondering, clueless mom was actually given to Jim, my husband and the father of our two daughters. And it was shared by another father. I was extremely blessed to be there when Jim's friend shared it, and I clung to its message while my girls were in their formative years and living at home. And guess what? I still draw comfort from it. Jim's mentor said, "The ground at the cross is level when it comes to child raising."

This experienced dad went on to explain that he had learned not to judge other parents because the way is hard for all mothers and fathers. It's a mega-challenge for each and every parent. He also said the end results are never fully evident because God is in the equation—that only time will reveal the outcome of our parenting, which is intermingled with God's sovereignty and grace. No matter what appears to be real, whether rough seas or smooth sailing, all parents need God, and with God, all things are always possible.

You know what this means, don't you? That you and I as parents must always be praying for our children regardless of their age or stage in life. In fact, this is yet another one of God's "missions for moms": We are to be prayer warriors. We are to do battle through prayer on behalf of our precious children.

My Prayer to Remember

Well, believe me, prayer continued after I said yes to tackling this book. In fact, the frequency and fervency of my talks with God escalated dramatically. Maybe the first prayer to burst forth from my heart was, "Oh, Lord, help me to remember! It's been a while since I had children at home day in and day out. Help me recall those early days of babies becoming toddlers, and toddlers becoming little girls...becoming school girls...becoming teens... becoming young adults."

My friend and fellow mom, the time span verbalized in my prayer covers several decades of mothering. As I paced and prayed and prayed and paced, an answer sparked in my brain: "Elizabeth, get out all of your old prayer journals! It's all there. You have a record of the kinds of things you were praying for when your girls were at home."

And that's exactly what I did. My years of recorded prayer requests—and their answers—showed me exactly what was going on in my two girls' lives at every stage of their development. And my prayer log also revealed what was going on in my heart and mind as well. Just holding my prayer notebook in my hands moved me to give fresh thanks to God for His availability and His provision of this awesome avenue of talking to Him. Through prayer I could share my emotions, fears, and problems with Him. And through prayer I could listen as He whispered encouragement, imparted His wisdom, and reminded me of His love for me—and my girls.

Thank goodness as a young mom I had a place—and a Person—to turn to with my worries, frustrations, failures, and needs. Prayer became my quiet sanctuary. Just stopping everything and making a decision or an appointment to set the concerns and busyness of life aside for a while so I could pray was and still is a calming step. It is a sort of time to inhale…and exhale, to center your attention on one thing—God and God alone. I always think of this step as doing what the psalmist referred to as coming "before His presence" (Psalm 100:2).

Yes, I know we are always in God's presence. I know He is omnipresent, everywhere all the time. And I know that I am never even for a split second out of His ever-watchful, ever-loving presence. We are never *not* in His immediate proximity. But to actually pause and think of entering into His presence, of coming boldly to His "throne of grace" (Hebrews 4:16), brings peace and power at the same time.

And you, too, have this same amazing resource of "God with you." He is always there, always waiting, always ready to listen, forgive, advise. He is ever available to comfort, encourage, instruct, strengthen, and guide. Whether you need to pour out your heart, emote, or get a pep talk, go to God. And don't forget to record your prayers and their answers. You think you won't forget, but write them down anyway. Do as the psalmist tells us—"forget not all His benefits," His blessings, His goodness (Psalm 103:2). Who knows, maybe one of these days I'll be reading your book of remembrance, your story recounting your experiences with God and His amazing answers to your prayers.

Ten Reasons Moms Don't Pray

With prayer being so critically important to us as moms and to the daughters we are trying to raise for God, wouldn't you think we would pray a lot more than we do? Have you thought about why you don't pray more? I'm sure you have. And so have I. In fact, as I looked at my own heart and prayer life, I discovered some reasons—and excuses—for not praying. This is my list. Maybe you'll find yourself there too, or come up with a few additions!

1. *Busyness*—Your days are filled with daily duties, while prayer is a spiritual duty. Solution? Because you are so busy, you must plan and schedule in what is truly important. Like David voiced to the Lord, "My voice you shall hear in the morning, O LORD; in the morning I will direct it to You" (Psalm 5:3). Your daughter's life and heart for God are an urgent priority that merits time—even first time—spent in the spiritual duty of prayer.

2. *Worldliness*—You live "in the world," which tends to squeeze you—and your daughter!—into its mold with its pressure, while prayer is a spiritual exercise. Solution? Turn your back on the world. "Do not love the world or the things in the world...For all that is in the world...is not of the Father but is of the world" (1 John 2:15-16). Instead, pray and "seek those things which are above.... Set your mind on things above, not on things of the earth" (Colossians 3:1-2).

3. *Foolishness*—Whenever you become overly consumed with what is foolish, trivial, and meaningless, you fail to pray. You begin to lose your ability to know the difference between what is good and what is evil. Between what is essential and that which has little eternal value. Everything becomes a "gray area" that doesn't require prayer. Or at least that's what you may think! Solution? "Seek first the kingdom of God and His righteousness" (Matthew 6:33).

4. *Distance*—You have no problem talking with your friends, and family, and those at work. But talk to someone outside your circle? No way—forget it! It's the same thing when it comes to talking to God. When you don't know God well enough, you don't feel like you can talk to Him. And what is He saying to you? "Come to Me" (Matthew 11:28)! "Draw near to God and He will draw near to you" (James 4:8).

5. *Ignorance*—You are clueless about how prayer works. And you don't understand or grasp God's goodness and His power, or His ability to provide for you "exceedingly abundantly above all that we ask or think" (Ephesians 3:20). So you don't pray. Solution? Be more faithful to learn about God from His Word, and memorize several of His promises—such as "God shall supply all your need" (Philippians 4:19).

6. *Sinfulness*—You don't pray because you know you've done something wrong, something that does not please God, something that goes against His Word. Solution? Keep short accounts with God. Deal with any sin issues as they comes up—on the spot—at the exact minute that you slip up and fail. Follow John's advice and confess your sins. The result? God forgives and purifies you (1 John 1:9). When King David finally, after about a year, confessed to God his sin with Bathsheba, the floodgates of communion with God were opened once again. Refuse to let sin become a barrier that keeps you from being able to pray for your daughter.

7. *Faithlessness*—You don't really believe in the power of prayer. You don't think prayer makes any difference. Therefore you don't pray. Solution? Remember that faith as small as a mustard seed has the power to move mountains (Matthew 17:20)—yours and your daughter's!

8. *Pridefulness*—Prayer shows your dependence on God. When you fail to pray, you are really saying that you don't have any needs. Or worse, you're saying, "No thank You, God. I've got this one. I'm good. I'll take care of this one myself. Your help is not required." Solution? Jesus put it this way: "Without Me you can do nothing" (John 15:5)—including raise a daughter after God's own heart!

9. *Inexperience*—We don't pray because...we don't pray! And because we don't pray, we don't know how to pray...so we don't pray. We are like a dog chasing after

its own tail. Solution? Start...and start now! Jesus said to "ask, and you will receive, that your joy may be full" (John 16:24). He gives you a simple formula of ASK—Ask, Seek, and Knock: "Ask, and it will be given to you; seek, and you will find; knock, and it will be opened to you" (Matthew 7:7). And in Jeremiah 33:3 God instructs you to "call to Me, and I will answer you, and show you great and mighty things, which you do not know."

10. *Laziness*—You're tired. Soooo tired. Too tired! But you're going to do it later, right? Yet you just never get around to it. Solution? Wait on the Lord. Pray! To those who do, God promises they "shall renew their strength; they shall mount up with wings like eagles, they shall run and not be weary, they shall walk and not faint" (Isaiah 40:31). Can you use any of this kind of power? Then you know what to do—pray!

Your Daughter Needs Your Prayers

I'm sure the list above is not new to you. I'm probably not saying anything you don't already know. You know you are supposed to pray, and you know you need to pray for all that's going on in your life. Wow, do you ever need this refuge and resource as a mom! But your daughter needs your prayers too. As her mother, you are the person closest to her. That's natural. That also means you, more than anyone else (along with God, of course), know best what troubles your precious girl. You are the one most savvy to her challenges, her friendships and friend-problems, her dreams and fears.

As early as her first year, your baby girl reaches out to you with her hands, which means, "Pick me up. I have a need." Just a few years later, she's running to you when she's afraid or hurt or excited about some wonderful thing and tells you all about it. When school days begin, she can't wait to get home each day and share her experiences with you. Junior high and high school open up all kinds of opportunities to talk about everything under the sun, from boyfriends, clothes, and makeup to drugs and sex, from first jobs and career planning to her goals and her qualms about her future.

On and on your mother-daughter bond has an opportunity to continue deepening as you move together through her dating and courtship experiences. And, if it is God's will, you and she will move through her engagement period, the planning of her wedding, and the births of her children.

How Do You View Your Prayer Life?

Well, I'm reminiscing and remembering all of these times and more. But it's time to stop pressing the fast-forward button. Let's talk about how a daughter of any age needs your prayers, mom, in every area of her tender and trying life. In short, she needs you to be a mother who prays. Whatever it takes, fight off any excuses and be that praying mom. View prayer as your unique privilege, and also your responsibility. Prayer is not a chore, but it does require a decision and some time. And it's not a job; it is your mission. And it's not optional. No, it's crucial. And here's why.

Prayer is not a chore, but it does require a decision and some time. And it's not a job; it is your mission.

To begin, view your responsibility to pray as a triangle. Here is you, Mom, represented by the dot below at the left:

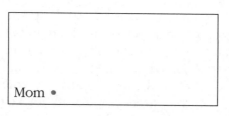

Then there is your daughter. She is symbolized by the dot over to the right:

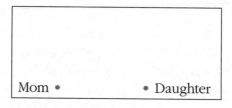

Above both you and your daughter—and ever in the center—is God

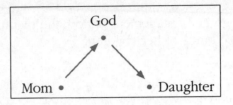

Now the war begins, as you desperately battle the forces of evil through prayer. There are important things you want for your daughter and are prepared to do fierce battle for:

- That she would come to believe in Christ.

- That she would desire to follow Jesus.

- That she would grow spiritually.

- That she would reflect Jesus in her character.

- That she would choose Christians as best friends.

- That she would desire to marry a Christian.

- That she would marry a Christian.

I also believe every one of these desires is what God wants because they come right out of His Word. In fact, He desires them even more than you do. But there is one glaring problem: You can't make your daughter do any of these things. You can't even make her want to do them. So you bring your appeals to God through prayer. You, in effect, point to your daughter and pray, "O Lord, please save my daughter. Move her heart to respond to Jesus." A mom can live out biblical truths (and she should). And a mom can talk about them (and she should). And a mom can even preach her heart out about them (and she should). But she cannot make spiritual truths a reality in her daughter's life. Only God is in charge of that reality. Only He can make this happen. Only He can move a heart. So...a mom must pray.

A Mom's Biggest Weapon

A mom after God's own heart has one big weapon in the spiritual battle for her daughter's heart: She can pray, and pray, and pray some more. She can be like the widow Jesus praised in one of His parables. This widow came before a judge repeatedly about a personal concern. The judge was reluctant to help her, but she persisted. Finally the judge gave her what she asked for, thinking, "Because this widow troubles me I will avenge her, lest by her continual coming she weary me" (Luke 18:5). Jesus commented, "Shall God not avenge His own elect who cry out day and night to Him, though He bears long with them? I tell you that He will avenge them speedily" (verses 7-8).

This passage is rich with meaning and messages. But one of Jesus' key messages to you as a mom is this: Just as the widow was persistent, you are to be constant in prayer and lift up your concerns for your daughter. Persist in prayer—for decades! Believe that God hears and God will answer. Don't ever give up; keep on asking. Our great, compassionate, loving Father does hear our prayers, our cries for help. And He will respond.

So I say, beg Him. Do battle in prayer. Humble yourself before the only One who can make a difference, the only One who can change a heart. Present your case, your petition, your plea. Keep on coming before God Almighty. Keep on asking, seeking, and knocking. Realize He and only He can accomplish the spiritual growth and transformation you are asking—begging!—for on behalf of a beloved daughter.

Going back to the triangle we looked at earlier, prayer involves...

- ⌐ a mom who desperately wants something for her daughter but cannot make it happen,

- ⌐ a daughter who desperately needs what her mom wants and may not even want it, and

- ⌐ a loving and almighty God who is the only One who can make it happen.

Are You Ready for the Challenge?

I cannot imagine a mom who is taking her time to read this

book who wouldn't do almost anything for her girl. And I know you are one of those caring moms, right? Well, what I'm about to ask isn't material. I'm not asking you to buy your daughter anything. That's too easy and, unfortunately, that's how most parents demonstrate their love. No, here it is: Are you ready to accept the challenge? The challenge to be a soldier of prayer for your daughter? Then dive into the next chapter for tips on becoming a prayer warrior for your daughter. But first, read the poem that follows. Then pray and ask God to make you this kind of mom—a mother who prays persistently for her daughter.

I Have a Mother Who Prays for Me

Some have had kings in their lineage,
Some to whom honor was paid.
Not blest of my ancestors—but,
I have a mother who prays.

I have a mother who prays for me
And pleads with the Lord every day for me.
Oh what a difference it makes for me—
I have a mother who prays.

Some have worldly success
And trust in riches they've made—
This is my surest asset,
I have a mother who prays.

My mother's prayers cannot save me,
Only mine can avail;
But mother introduced me to Someone—
Someone who never could fail.

Oh yes…I have a mother who prays for me
And pleads with the Lord every day for me.
Oh what a difference it makes for me—
I have a mother who prays.

—AUTHOR UNKNOWN

Chapter 2

The Prayer Warrior

Part 2—Gearing Up for Battle

We do not wrestle against flesh and blood,
but against principalities, against powers,
against the rulers of the darkness of this age,
against spiritual hosts of wickedness
in the heavenly places.
—EPHESIANS 6:12

What am I doing here?! I wondered. *How did this happen? I never bargained for this!*

But there I was, standing breathless after hiking up a very steep and long trail to reach the windswept plateau of Masada. This ancient fortress of the Jews in Israel overlooked the Dead Sea some 1300 feet below. Together with a group of seminary students lead by my husband, Jim, we had climbed to the top of this rich historical site. Jim had invited me to come to Israel with him as he co-led the student group. They came to grow in their knowledge of biblical history. But I went to search the land and context in which the woman of Proverbs 31 lived. If you've read my book *Beautiful in God's Eyes,* you know that I discovered some things about her roots, making me realize all the more how amazing she was!

One of the interesting facts about this woman is that she's described by God as "a virtuous wife" (Proverbs 31:10). The word "virtuous" is used 200-plus times in the Bible to describe an army. It is used in reference to a man of war, men of war, and men prepared for war. And appropriately enough, our P-31 lady was a warrior when it came to mental toughness and physical energy.

What Does It Take to Become a Prayer Warrior?

With this mental picture of the woman and mom from Proverbs 31 in your mind, read the words in Ephesians 6:12, which appear on the first page of this chapter. Meet your enemy—and your daughter's enemy! Prayer is not just a nice little thing to do as a mom. It's not meant to give you a warm, fuzzy feeling. No, it's warfare against the powers of darkness and evil. So let me ask you: What would you do, or give, or give up to be an effective prayer warrior on behalf of your daughter? To be a tough fighter for the life and soul of your daughter requires two things of you right away.

Guard Your Walk with God

First, you need to guard your walk with God. By this I mean a mom after God's own heart must be willing to give up whatever does not please God, whatever goes against His Word and His will, whatever is sin of any kind and any size. Whether minuscule or massive on humankind's scale, in God's economy, sin is sin—period. It interrupts your walk with Him, your communication with Him, your fellowship with Him, your ability to effectively pray for your daughter. God asks that we love and obey Him first, and then ask Him in prayer for what's important.

I'll never forget the day I realized that I could not simply rush to God and barge into His presence if things were not right in my walk with Him. It became brilliantly clear that I couldn't ask anything of Him until I first asked for His forgiveness. Then I could ask for His help concerning my daughters.

From cover to cover, we see in the Bible how crucial our walk with God is. He tells us in James 4:8 to put away all sin, to cleanse our hands and lives of sin, and to purify our hearts. In short, He tells us not to pray until and unless we obey. The psalmist knew this principle. He wrote, "If I regard iniquity in my heart, the Lord will not hear" (Psalm 66:18). And Solomon put it this way: "One who turns away his ear from hearing the law, even his prayer is an abomination" (Proverbs 28:9).

One scholar explained, "If we refuse to repent, if we harbor and cherish certain sins, then a wall is placed between us and God...Our attitude toward life should be one of confession and obedience."[8]

But here is welcomed news! If the desire of our heart is to follow God by tending to our walk with Him, He delights in listening to our prayers. The apostle Peter assures us "the eyes of the LORD are on the righteous, and His ears are open to their prayers" (1 Peter 3:12).

And here's another teaching that hit home with me (I'm so glad it did!). It was something one of my former pastors constantly reminded his congregation: "Put away your favorite sins. Greater things are at stake." Wow! Greater things are hanging in the balance, like my daughters' salvation, my daughters' choices! When we moms don't maintain a right relationship with the Lord, it's possible for our daughter's relationship with God to suffer simply because we cannot pray effectively for her. Our own sin causes us to be disqualified and ineffective as her prayer warrior. Sin silences our voice and voids our requests lifted to God on our daughter's behalf. So God's message to us is to guard our walk with Him—to get rid of sin and get on our knees. Greater things are at stake!

Give Up Some Time

Second, being a tough fighter for your daughter will require you to give up some time. It's absolutely true that whatever is important to us will require our time and attention. And praying for your daughter is definitely a top priority. She is your flesh and blood, as close to being your clone as anything or anyone will ever come. So you will need to give up some of the time you spend doing secondary things to buy time for the primary thing—that is, praying for your daughter. Somehow, somewhere, you've got to find some time. The Bible refers to this trade-off of lesser things for the greater things as "redeeming the time" (Ephesians 5:16).

When it comes to you and your daughter, God has given you an allotted "season" with her right under your roof and under your wings, and it will truly fly by! So make the most of your time with her now. And that includes taking time to pray for her.

Here's a quick exercise you can do to make that happen—it's one I go through almost every day. Think about how much time you spend each day watching the news, or a favorite program, or even the Weather Channel. Or how about the amount of time you put into exercise? Or online shopping or banking, sending tweets, going on Facebook, or e-mailing family, friends, and associates? When you add up all of this daily expenditure of your golden minutes and hours, you'll realize that you definitely have time for prayer—especially prayer for your daughter's life and soul. When you weigh how you spend so much of your time against how much time you spend praying for your daughter, the picture is frightfully clear.

Oh, it's not that there's necessarily anything wrong with spending time in these ways. These kinds of activities keep us in touch, inform us, help us take care of others and our finances, even educate us and give us pleasure or a nice break. But think about adding one more thing into your time—something that's way more important than these activities. Think about adding in prayer for yourself, for your family, your ministries, your church and, most especially for your priceless daughter.

And go another step and make prayer first on your list of priorities for the day. Then stand back and watch God's blessings pour in! To begin, you are blessed. You benefit because when you pray, you are putting God first. You change and grow as you talk to God. And, blessing upon blessing, when you pray for your daughter, she benefits. She is blessed. To "daughterize" a famous quote, "There is nothing that makes us love a daughter so much as praying for her."[9]

A Personal Story

I had to learn to make the choice to pray first. Yes, doing that couldn't be more simple, but it is oh so hard! I discovered that it takes little or no effort to get into a comfortable, fun, even productive groove in my daily life. And it's even easier to get into a groove of bad habits. But I was trying to get into a God groove—a groove of being a mom after God's own heart. And I knew in my heart this key choice to pray, and pray for my daughters, was right—and needed. But, probably like you, there were always 1000 things to do and 1001 ways to spend my time...and 1002 excuses for not getting around to prayer! The only solution was to do it—just do it, and do it first. So at my first opportunity each day, I talked to God about my girls, my princesses.

Depending on their ages and issues, I prayed for their health and their friends, or that they would make some friends. I prayed for their obedience to Jim and me, that they would respond to discipline. I prayed for the list I shared a few pages back—their salvation, their love for God, their spiritual growth, their safety, and their time at church events and camps. I worked my way through my growing prayer list day by day.

Remember our motto: You can do it! You will find your way, I promise you. Step 1 is to believe that praying for your daughter is vital. And Step 2 is to sit down and simply begin. Pray! It can be as elementary as, "Good morning, God. I'm Rebecca, and I'm here to talk to you about my daughter Molly." And off you go!

Now for some weapons training. Read on!

Be Specific When You Pray

Here's a thought to chew on—a thought that sank its teeth into my soul when I read it! "Much of our praying is just asking God to bless someone that is ill and to keep us plugging along. But prayer is not merely prattle: it is warfare."[10] The message is this: When it's time to pray, it's time to go to war! This means that as a prayer warrior, you don't just prattle. You do battle for what's deadly serious in your daughter's life. For instance...

Your Daughter's Commitment to Christ

We've already agreed that a mom who loves the Lord with all her heart wants, above all else, for her daughter (and all her children) to belong to Christ and have a committed, vibrant love for Him. Therefore, as such a mom, your living and all of your parenting points your girl to God. And so do your prayers. Your daughter's relationship with God is almost always the first prayer you lift up to God as you pray each day for her. If you're like me, your thoughts go something like this: "Lord, save my daughter! If You choose to answer only one prayer of mine, please, Lord, let it be this one!"

Right this minute I'm looking at some of my prayer journal pages from the past. Immediately my eyes fell on this prayer request. It's listed on my page of "general" daily prayer requests for both of my daughters—that they would "desire to read the Word and grow and pray." My part, both then and now, was and is to faithfully live out my love for the Lord in front of my daughters and to pray that they grow to possess an even greater love for Him. God's role, then and now, was and is to work in their hearts.

Your Daughter's Spiritual Growth

Just this week the pastor of the church Jim and I were attending devoted his entire message to the importance of the Bible in our spiritual growth. He said God has given us several remarkable gifts—His Son, salvation through His Son, and His Word. He explained that Jesus came to make salvation possible, salvation through Jesus makes us children of God, and God's Word teaches us and helps us to know God and live according to His will.

You are God's go-to person for your daughter, Number One on His list as someone who prays for her.

When it comes to your daughter's spiritual growth, your prayers are vital. She needs to be saved from her sins, which only a relationship with Jesus, God's Son, can accomplish. And she needs to hear and know what the Bible teaches so that, by God's grace, she can avoid many of the mistakes most girls make while growing up and instead, live in obedience to God.

So what can you do? Pray and act! Did you just find out you are expecting? Then start praying. And from your daughter's Day 1 appearance on earth, read and verbalize God's Word to her in her newborn state. Commit yourself to doing what God tells parents to do—to talk about the Lord from sunup to sundown.

As time and your daughter's life move forward, keep praying.

Be ever the prayer warrior. And make it a goal to provide Christian resources for her at each learning level. See that she has a little cloth Bible with some key verses and illustrations in it to "read" while she's in her crib or car seat. Then promote her to a simple picture Bible. Then, of course, move her on to a "real" Bible, as my granddaughter calls a Bible without illustrations. And, in time, give her a study Bible that will help her understand God's truth in greater depth and fuel her growth as a Christian.

Your Daughter's Physical Development and Health

Talk about an area where girls suffer—and their moms too! Physical and health issues are a perpetually challenging part of life for girls and women of all ages. What little baby doesn't love looking over your shoulder into a mirror and laughing at the image? It seems once we've had that first look in the mirror, from then on we are obsessed with every aspect of our physical being. As we grow up, our teeth change (here come the braces!). Our skin changes (how do you get rid of acne?). Our bodies change. Which means our emotions change. Which means our attitudes change. Oh, and our appetites grow (how does a kid lose a few pounds?).

And, mom, as you well know, you are right there in the middle of these trying times. You are God's go-to person for your daughter, Number One on His list as someone who prays for her. You are possibly the only person she can talk to when it comes to matters of a more personal nature. So your mission is to nurture the kind of loving and affirming relationship with her that will cause her to come to you, knowing you care, that you'll help, that you'll understand, and above all else, that you'll love her no matter what, even when she feels like she's an ugly duckling or she thinks she's terribly awkward.

And as your daughter is going through these periods of self-doubt, you can pray. As her prayer warrior, can pray for wisdom to help her understand and accept that what's happening to her physically is all part of God's beautiful plan for her life. Your job is also to pray for her—and with her—about the importance of inner beauty over physical appearance.

You Can Do It!

Each of the following suggestions is something you can do to contribute toward becoming the mom you dream of being. And each one betters your life...and your daughter's too. Here we go:

Check your heart.

Being a mom after God's own heart is a matter of where your heart is at. We'll get to praying for your daughter, but first pray about your heart and its spiritual condition. That's why prayer is so important for a mom. It's a spiritual discipline. When you pray, you are acknowledging that God is an active participant in your life, and your daughter's too. Taking time each day to pray will strengthen your spiritual life, which, in turn, will strengthen your relationship with your daughter and her relationship with God.

Ask God for wisdom.

There's not a mom anywhere who doesn't want to do whatever she can to advise and direct her daughter, and you're one of them, right? And like these moms, you know you need help. That's why James 1:5 is a real encouragement. I call it Mom's Go-to Verse: "If any of you lacks wisdom, let him ask of God...and it will be given to him." If you feel as bewildered about motherhood as I've felt over the years, you'll pray day and night for wisdom from God about how to raise a daughter after His own heart. Just know that when you go to God and ask Him for wisdom, you've gone to the right place. As the verse from James says, wisdom "will be given." Once you ask, it's on the way!

Make a prayer list for your daughter.

If you're not careful, your prayers for your daughter can become general or even rote, leaving you muttering vague requests like "God, please bless my daughter today." Your daughter has specific issues she faces each day and at each stage of her life. So develop a prayer list or book just for her. Record your specific concerns. Add her prayer requests to it. And add new issues as they come along. Then bring these specific concerns before God. (Jim and I prayed for godly mates for our girls, if marriage was God's will for them. We lifted this specific prayer to God almost daily for close to 20 years, before Jim walked each of our daughters down the aisle to marry their two Pauls in answer to our prayers.)

Refuse to miss a day.

With a busy schedule, it's possible to end up going several days without praying for your daughter. There's just so much to do! But here's a thought: "Time spent in prayer will yield more than that given to work."[11] That's especially true where your daughter is concerned! And here's another thought: If you aren't praying for your daughter each day, who is? Maybe a godly grandparent or your husband? I hope so. But it's possible that on any given day, you are the only one praying for your daughter. So don't let a no-one-prayed-for-my-daughter day happen! Your daughter needs your prayers, every day, come what may. Every busy mom can somehow find five or ten minutes in her day. So find them...and pray. The stakes are much too high for you to fail to spend some time in prayer for your precious daughter.

Mom's Think Pad

Before you move on to your next Mom Mission, take a minute or two to think about what you can do to track with God as a mom. Make some plans of your own to take a few small steps that make a big difference.

1. I know I don't pray as much as I should. And I'm far from being a prayer warrior for my dear sweet precious wonderful daughter. What are several ways to turn up the heat on my prayer life? And what can I do to follow through on my good intentions?

2. I need to set up a prayer list or journal for my daughter. When will I sit down and take care of this? I'm going to put it on my calendar right now. It's a date!

3. What are the three most important things in my daughter's life that need my immediate prayer attention?

4. Is my daughter really a Christian? When can I talk with her about her relationship with Jesus? And when will I start storming the gates of heaven with my prayers?

5. As I think about my girl's future, what's vital? I've got to put that on my prayer list (or in my prayer journal) right away. The future is now!

Chapter 3

The Sower of Seed

Part 1—The Heart of a Sower

The sower sows the word.
—MARK 4:14

lashback! I'm sitting at my writing desk recalling my young mommy days. There I was—a brand-new baby Christian with two toddling girls...and a Bible. I was desperately trying to find out what God had to say to me as one of His moms so I could begin doing whatever He said to do. What I had been doing (which most of the time was nothing—just letting things go) definitely wasn't working. I needed help, and I knew it. So I turned in my Bible to my favorite "mom verses"— Deuteronomy 6:6-7. It was there I found out exactly what I, the mother of two little daughters, needed to do. According to these verses, it was a matter of my heart. I, the mom, was to make sure God's Word was in my heart. Why? So I could "teach" His precepts and "talk" about them to my girls day and night in every life situation. I knew I needed to do that. *But how, oh how?* I wondered.

A Recipe for Sharing God's Truth

What I soon discovered was a sort of recipe for sharing biblical truth with my little ones who, of course, grew to be bigger! A few daily actions—and decisions—from a mom's heart help get the teaching and talking job done.

Preach the Word

Moms, like preachers, are to preach, teach, and share God's Word with their daughters. It's a little like what the apostle Paul told his young preaching protégé, Timothy—"preach the word!" (2 Timothy 4:2). In other words, a preacher must preach. It's a role, a responsibility, a stewardship given by God. And speaking the Word of God is another of our missions as moms.

Being a "preaching mom" is also something I learned from Ruth Graham, the wife of evangelist Billy Graham and the mother of five children (three of them daughters). In the biography of her famous husband, I read about an interview in which Ruth was asked her opinion on her role as mother and homemaker. She replied, "To me, it's the nicest, most rewarding job in the world second in importance to none, not even preaching." Then she added, "Maybe it is preaching!"[12]

Now apply this to yourself as a mom with a precious daughter who needs to hear God's Word preached! And when I say "preach," please know that I don't mean finger pointing, a raised voice, or thumping your fist on a Bible. I simply mean being on guard for every opportunity to share God's truth. And, when they arrive, share naturally. Don't hold back.

Be persistent. There's plenty to worry about as a mom, but here's one thing you never have to fret about: Don't ever think sharing biblical truth isn't all that important, that it doesn't really make a difference. No, think exactly the opposite! God says "the word of God is living and powerful, and sharper than any two-edged sword, piercing even to the division of soul and spirit, and of joints and marrow, and is a discerner of the thoughts and intents of the heart" (Hebrews 4:12).

This description from God Himself of the power and effects of His Word should encourage you to take every opportunity to share it with your daughter. It's got to be passed on, and it's got to flow out of a conscious effort on your part. That's what Billy Graham found out. This man of God realized he needed to create opportunities to share God's truth. So in the early days of his ministry and fame, he made a decision to mention the Lord every time he signed an autograph for someone. He made a decision to turn every interview toward the gospel message. Writing to his wife Ruth, Billy reported, "I have decided in businessmen's luncheons to go all out for the gospel. I am not going to give a talk on world events or give them sweet little lullabies."[13]

Mom, make a note to self: "I have decided...to go all out for the gospel."

Become Like a Farmer

Maybe picturing yourself as a preacher of sorts is a little overwhelming for you. But seeing yourself as being like a farmer probably isn't so hard. Hmmm, let's see. A farmer gets up early...and so does a mom! A farmer does hard physical labor...and so does a mom. A farmer works long hours...and so does a mom. A farmer falls into bed at night, totally exhausted...and so does a mom.

Well, Jesus taught a parable that shows us one more thing a farmer does, as well as a mom: A farmer sows seed, and so does a mom. Before we dive into how you are to be a sower of seed, read through Jesus' Parable of the Sower. Just read it, and enjoy it. It's found in Mark 4:3-8 (and Luke 8:5-8).

> Listen! Behold, a sower went out to sow. And it happened, as he sowed, that some seed fell by the wayside; and the birds of the air came and devoured it. Some fell on stony ground, where it did not have much earth; and immediately it sprang up because it had no depth of earth. But when the sun was up it was scorched, and because it had no root it withered away. And some seed fell among thorns; and the thorns grew up and choked it, and it yielded no crop. But other seed fell on good ground and yielded a crop that sprang up, increased and produced: some thirtyfold, some sixty, and some a hundred (Mark 4:3-8).

Are you wondering what all of this means? Well, you're not alone. In fact, you are in good company! When the 12 disciples were alone with Jesus after He told this very story, they asked Him the same question. Read on for the Lord's explanation:

> The sower sows the word. And these are the ones by the wayside where the word is sown. When they hear, Satan comes immediately and takes away the word that was sown in their hearts. These likewise are the ones sown on stony ground who, when they hear the word, immediately receive it with gladness; and they have no root in themselves, and so endure only for a time. Afterward, when tribulation or persecution arises for the word's sake, immediately they stumble. Now these are the ones sown among thorns; they are the ones who hear the word, and the cares of this world, the deceitfulness of riches, and the desires for other things entering in choke the word, and it becomes unfruitful. But these are the ones sown on good ground, those who hear the word, accept it, and bear fruit: some thirtyfold, some sixty, and some a hundred (4:14-20).

This is a lot to take in! But I wanted you to read the entire parable before we focus on your part in God's plan for you as a mother—that you are to be a sower of seed. It's vital that you realize you have to make a conscious decision to speak God's Word to your daughter. You need to become like the farmer in Jesus' parable, who purposefully "went out to sow." He decided to get out of bed and go out and do the work of sowing. And, like him, you'll want to make the same decision to get up each day and go out and purposefully plant the seeds of truth on the soil of your daughter's heart.

Of course, you'll want to sing silly songs and sweet little lullabies to your young ones, and continue doing fun things with them as they get bigger. That's a good thing! But don't forget to be faithful to sow God's Word as well. Like the farmer in Jesus' story, make a deliberate effort to sow the seed. And like Billy Graham, be willing to go all out for the gospel. Your mission as a mom is to actively sow the seed—and pray, pray, pray. Pray that, by

God's grace, your daughter's heart responses will be positive and accepting of God's gospel of salvation and the truths of the Bible.

The Elements Needed to Produce a Harvest

You've probably had some experience with gardening. Maybe you don't have a green thumb, but you love trying! So I'm guessing by now you know there are a few essentials that are needed before you can enjoy a potted plant...or an acre of roses. Every gardener needs seed or a seedling, rich soil, mulch, fertilizer, and water to achieve the desired result—beautiful, healthy plants. From Jesus' parable we learn about the elements needed to produce a spiritual harvest.

> *God's moms are to be "teachers of good things," especially the good things in the Bible.*

The Seed

First, you must have seed. To apply Jesus' parable to yourself as a mom, realize that the seed Jesus mentioned is, as He explained, "the word" (verse 14), "the word of God" (Luke 8:11). Jesus is referring to the gospel message of salvation—the message that every person is a sinner and can receive God's forgiveness of sin through Christ's death on the cross. Jesus explained that the farmer—or sower—is anyone who takes the time to plant the good seed of Scripture into the lives of others. God's Word is perfectly good and it helps you to accomplish the assignment given to you in Titus 2:3—God's moms are to be "teachers of good things," especially the good things in the Bible.

What does it take to be a sower of seed? Obviously it requires seed—the Word. Scripture must be in your mind, in your heart, and on your lips. I know some women whose every word gives evidence of this inner condition. God sent one of these women—a former Campus Crusade for Christ worker—into my life. She never failed to share God's Word in every encounter. Maybe it was something from her devotions that day, and she was so excited about what she had read that she couldn't help herself. She couldn't keep from passing it on! Or maybe it was the verse she was memorizing, and it was so rich and full and transforming that she couldn't hold it in. Or after she asked me (and everyone else she met) for any prayer requests, she shared a verse of encouragement related to the need. It was easy. It was natural. It was never threatening. It was simply the lovely overflow of the treasure of God's Word stored up in her heart. She was always able to "speak a word in season" (Isaiah 50:4)—a word that was timely, appropriate, positive, uplifting. She couldn't help it! She was a living example of Jesus' principle that "out of the abundance of the heart the mouth speaks" (Matthew 12:34).

Think of all the things you talk about in a day—things that take up time and choke out your opportunity for sharing God's Word, things that have no value, things that fail to edify and encourage. How much better to be excited and filled with God's Word—filled to the point that it spills out on everyone around you, especially—and beginning with—your daughter!

The Sower

After you fill your seed bag (that's your heart) with the seed (that's the Word of God), Jesus' next instruction is for you to sow away...and to sow liberally! This too requires a deliberate decision each day to be a mom who sows the seed upon her daughter's heart.

This is exactly the next message of Jesus' parable. Before you can enjoy a harvest, there must be a sower. There has to be! Why? Because seed is seed. And seed can sit in a bag or a box—or a heart—for ages. But that seed is dynamite! It is the Word of God, living and powerful. It works on a person's heart, attitudes, thoughts, and motives like nothing else. It examines, judges, and admonishes hearers to believing faith and holy living. It is truly the Word of power!

So, God has given you, the mother to your daughter, the seed, His Word—the dynamite. He has entrusted it to you. Yet not one seed will ever take root and work its miracle of salvation until it is actively sown. Therefore, you, mom, must be the sower of the powerful, precious, life-changing, able-to-save seed. Yes, it's true God will send other wonderful people who sow the seed of His

Word into your daughter's heart as she passes through life. Godly Sunday school teachers, Bible club leaders, youth leaders, Christian writers, schoolteachers, and other Christian girls and their moms—and, of course, caring, praying grandmothers—will sow the seed God has given them to sow. But you, mom, are the primary sower of God's gospel of saving grace and forgiveness.

And here's a zinger from the Bible that will hopefully encourage you in your commitment to sow the seed of truth into your daughter's soul. It's a truth, a fact, and a promise from God, all rolled up into one, that confirms to us the power of God's Word:

> For as the rain comes down, and the snow from heaven, and do not return there, but water the earth, and make it bring forth and bud, that it may give seed to the sower and bread to the eater, so shall My word be that goes forth from My mouth; it shall not return to Me void, but it shall accomplish what I please, and it shall prosper in the thing for which I sent it (Isaiah 55:10-11).

If you find yourself being hesitant, feeling unsure, or thinking that sharing biblical truth isn't all that important or popular, be sure you zero in on the fact that every truth out of God's Word that you share with your daughter counts. Not one truth is ever wasted, or powerless, or unimportant, or fruitless. Every truth contributes positively to God's will and purposes in the life of the hearer—your daughter!

A Pep Talk for Moms

So how's your heart? Are you sowing seeds of God's love and His truth into your daughter's heart? It's never too early and it's never too late to start. That's because God's Word cannot return void, no matter when it's sown. It always works on the heart of the hearer and accomplishes God's will.

And realize too that something is better than nothing. At first it may be a little hard or feel awkward or forced to quote a scripture, or share a proverb, or state a biblical principle. If this happens, you'll have to determine to do what God is asking of you anyway. You'll have to remind yourself to be on your toes for natural opportunities that come along each day as you and your daughter sit, walk, lie down, and rise up. And, as Billy Graham shared, if the opportunities don't appear to be there, create them!

We moms cannot underestimate the urgency of planting God's truth in our daughters' hearts and minds, no matter what their age. They need a relationship with God. And His Word stimulates, promotes, and can bring about this relationship (2 Timothy 2:15).

Your daughter needs the knowledge and strength God's truth and wisdom provide for making it through life. And you, her mom, have the supreme privilege of partnering with God to, Lord willing, make your daughter's spiritual birth and development into a woman after God's own heart a reality.

I realize the verse I'm about to share has to do with the manner in which we practice the stewardship of our money, but "the principle of sowing and reaping" also happens to apply to sowing the seed of God's truth into your daughter's heart: "He who sows sparingly will also reap sparingly, and he who sows bountifully will also reap bountifully" (2 Corinthians 9:6).

The Sower of Seed

Part 2—The Work of a Sower

A sower went out to sow...
—LUKE 8:5

For years, my Jim taught goal-setting seminars. His first aim for his groups was to bring them to the point of setting personal goals they could own and be committed to. Once the men and women made it to this point in the workshop, Jim then taught how they could devise a plan for moving toward their goals—what they needed to do to prepare themselves, and what action steps they needed to take.

Well, God has set the goals for you and me as moms of daughters. And one of those goals is to sow the seed of His Word into the soil of our girls' hearts. But how?

Sowing Involves Planning and Preparation

For answers to the But how? question, let's revisit the farmer in Jesus' parable to glean a few more insights from him. To bring us up to speed, we already know that to sow seed, the farmer must first ensure that he has a store of seed to sow. That's a goal.

Then follows the planning and preparation necessary to make this goal of possessing seed a reality. In Jesus' story, the seed does not just magically appear. His teaching is not a fairy tale. No, to have seed on hand when planting time comes around requires that the farmer plan ahead—about one year ahead, because each time seed is harvested, a portion must be held back for the next crop.

So obviously, to achieve the goal of having seed to plant, a farmer must abide by a schedule. That's because there's a right time to sow, a season for sowing, a time when weather and soil conditions are ideal for sowing the seed.

And preparation is a must. The soil has to be prepared. It must be plowed to create furrows that catch the seed and the rain. The farmer's one-year calendar includes tasks like harvesting the crop, setting aside seed for the next crop, preparing the fields, and sowing the seed.

So, what does your mothering schedule look like? As you create it, remember the goal—to raise a daughter after God's own heart. What activities will help this process along? What planning and preparation must you carry out? Write these things down and put them on your daily schedule, your to-do list.

For instance, each day you'll want to gather fresh seed from God's Word.

Then you'll need to remember to sow it at every opportunity.

Next comes watching over the day, the seed, and the soil of your daughter's heart with vigilant prayer as a faithful laborer. As Jesus urged His disciples, "Pray the Lord of the harvest to send out laborers into His harvest" (Matthew 9:38). Whether you realize it or not, you are a laborer God has sent to work in the field of your daughter's heart. You are a key part in the answer to your own prayers!

And don't forget, the work of sowing seed is a repetitious act. The farmer does it year after year. And so will you! Day after day and year after year, you'll be sowing God's Word. And sowing is methodical work. You have to

    —plan for it (make a point to purposefully share God's Word),

    —schedule it (set a time for a quiet time with your girl),

    —store up the grain for sowing (spend personal time in Bible reading and study),

—plow and prepare the field (do all things concerning your daughter with a heart of love), and then

—walk the furrows of soil ("walk" through your day, as Deuteronomy 6:7 says), and

—broadcast handful after handful of precious seed, deliberately and liberally ("talk" about God's Word, again, as Deuteronomy 6:7 says).

Sowing Involves Work

For decades my uncle farmed 20 sections of land (that's 12,800 acres or 20 square miles) in the Texas Panhandle. I never could get over how hard he worked! His work never let up. There were no weeks or weekends off, no winter vacations in Florida. He got up at 4:00 a.m. seven days a week to begin his chores. Then he came in for a hearty farmer's breakfast—then out again for more backbreaking chores. After a large lunch my uncle had a nap in his favorite chair with his classic Stetson hat resting over his face and his booted feet up on a footstool. Then he got up again and worked until dark, ending the day with dinner and a very early bedtime.

Few things in life could ever be as grand as seeing your daughter love and follow the Lord.

Are you relating as a mom? Both a mom and a farmer are up early. Both work hard all day, and both fall into bed at the end of the day, exhausted! Anything as critical and urgent as nurturing your daughter's heart and life demands—and deserves—your all-out effort. My favorite rhyme in my children's book *God's Wisdom for Little Girls* is "God's Little Girl Is Busy."

The garden of God's little girl—how grand!
It began with a dream, a prayer, and a plan.
Nothing this splendid just happens, we know:
It takes time and care for flowers to grow.[14]

And it's true! Nothing grand just happens. And that includes raising a daughter after God's own heart. It takes time, work, care, and prayer for seed to be sown. Then, Lord willing, as you put in more time, work, care, and prayer, the seed will take root in your precious one's heart and grow to blossom and bear fruit. When you think about it, few things in life could ever be as grand as seeing your daughter love and follow the Lord. Surely that's worth any amount of work!

Sowing Involves Patience

King Solomon, also known as "the Preacher," wrote, "To everything there is a season, a time for every purpose under heaven… a time to plant, and a time to pluck what is planted" (Ecclesiastes 3:1-2). He was telling us that there is a time to sow and a time to reap, a time to plant and a time to harvest. This implies that there is a waiting period in between these steps. So what can a mom be doing while waiting, waiting for God's work to be done in her daughter's soul? Here are a few vital projects.

Protect Your Daughter

Once a farmer prepares the field and sows the seed, he must protect his crop, his little fledgling sprouts. If a torrential rain threatens, he places sandbags and barriers around the field to keep runaway waters from washing away his budding plants. And if birds are a problem, he positions a scarecrow in his field to deter them from feeding upon the seeds in the ground.

Like the farmer, your job is to prepare, plan, and sow the seed—and then wait patiently for the results. And while you are waiting, your duty is to watch over your field, your daughter and her heart. You are to be like the woman in Proverbs 31:27: "She watches over the ways of her household, and does not eat the bread of idleness." I remember reading a scholar's comments that this "watcher woman" had eyes in the back of her head! Like her, you need to fiercely watch, care, and act on anything and everything that might endanger your "crop"—your daughter and the work of the seed of the Word in her heart.

Know What's Going on in Your Daughter's Life

While you wait on God's Word to work in your daughter's soul, you are also to do what another proverb advises: "Be diligent to know the state of your flocks, and attend to your herds" (Proverbs 27:23). While you wait on evidence of spiritual life and the miracle of salvation in your girl, stay super busy praying and watching, guarding and protecting your "flocks" and "herds"—your daughter, your children. Is your daughter healthy? How is she spending her time? What's going on at school? And who are her friends?

Your Job Is to Sow the Seed

Are you sowing enthusiastically, faithfully, and in faith? You must believe in what you are doing. And you must believe in the power of the Word to break a will, save a heart, and transform a soul. And above all, don't get discouraged. Your daughter may hear some of the truths you share and not hear others. She may understand some of what you say, but not all of it. She may say, "Oh Mom, not again." Or, "Can we do this later?" Hopefully she'll even get to the stage where she says, "I know what you're going to say, Mom. I've heard it a thousand times." (And by the way, mom, this is great news! It means you are speaking up, and what you are saying is being remembered and etched upon her heart. It means the truths you are sowing cannot be shaken off by your daughter in years to come.)

Reaping Involves God

In the end, a mom after God's own heart must trust God. He is the One who determines everything, which includes the outcome of your parenting efforts and the timing of events. Think about the farmer's crop. To sprout, grow, and thrive to maturity, seeds and seedlings need rain, sun, and dry heat. Only God can bring forth and create these conditions. In the parable of the mustard seed, Jesus taught, "This is what the kingdom of God is like. A man scatters seed on the ground. Night and day, whether he sleeps or gets up, the seed sprouts and grows, though he does not know how.

All by itself the soil produces grain—first the stalk, then the head, then the full kernel in the head" (Mark 4:26-28 NIV).

Once again, like a farmer, we moms are to obediently and diligently sow the seed of truth. And we are to watch over, pray over, and protect the precious seed. And then we are to wait to see what God will do, because He's the only One who can orchestrate time and events and conditions…and save a soul, including your daughter's.

There will be days—maybe even years or decades—when you see no evidence of fruit from your labors. But you cannot let anything cause you to stop doing what God asks. So sow the seed. And keep on sowing the seed. Sow bountifully, abundantly, and confidently! "Season" your dear daughter's heart with the salt of truth. And never stop, no matter what. As a favorite mothering verse of mine says, "Let your speech always be with grace, seasoned with salt" (Colossians 4:6). The apostle Paul wrote these words immediately after he asked others to pray that God would open a door for him to speak of Christ.

That's not a bad prayer to pray for ourselves, is it? Share the Lord verbally with your daughter, and pray. And do as Psalm 37:7 advises: "Rest in the LORD, and wait patiently for Him." Only God can open a mind and heart and transform a life. Pray that God will open your daughter's heart and the seed will take root and produce spiritual life.

Sowing Involves Faith

Like the farmer who is diligent to sow seed so that there might be crops, you and I, Mom, must wake up each and every day and sow God's life-giving seed into our daughters' hearts. That's your part. And God's part is to produce the harvest, to move your daughter's heart and bring her to a full knowledge of His Son, Jesus Christ. So rest in the Lord and wait patiently for Him in faith, knowing that He will do His part perfectly and in His timing. God is completely sovereign. He knows all things and is in control of all things, including how and when He will transform your daughter's heart. Remember, the timing of the harvest is in God's hands (Psalm 31:15).

When you find yourself worrying, don't! Don't get impatient if time is passing and your little girl is growing up and has not yet experienced personal faith in Christ. And don't compare how God is choosing to work in your daughter's life to His plan for her friends' hearts, or in your other children's lives. The timing is totally up to God. You cannot "make" salvation happen. You can only do your part in faith. You can only sow the seed. Then you can pray in faith...and then rest in faith.

———————— *You Can Do It!* ————————

Each of the following suggestions is something you can do to contribute toward becoming the mom you dream of being. And each one betters your life...and your daughter's too. Here we go:

Develop a closer walk with Jesus.

Have you ever noticed that people like to talk about who and what they know? If they're big TV watchers, you'll hear about the latest television shows. If they have a hobby, prepare yourself to hear all about it. Well, the closer you walk with Jesus, the more you will want to talk about Him to your daughter. If you want your daughter to know and love Jesus, then you, as the one closest to her, must introduce her to your best Friend and help her get to know Him as her best Friend too.

Make the most of every opportunity to talk about Jesus.

Open your eyes. The opportunities are there. For instance, put your daughter's weekly Sunday school Bible paper to use. Don't just glance at it when she hands it to you as you're leaving church. Or worse, don't dare throw it away! Take it home and use it as an opportunity to discuss spiritual truth. Sure, you can place it on the refrigerator door, but more than that, be sure it goes into your daughter's heart. One way you can do that is by using it for your little one's devotions. Let her see that you and her teacher at church think this information is very important and special. Help your daughter create a notebook for saving all of her Sunday school papers. Make it a cool art and craft project you do together. Then date each lesson. Punch holes in the pages, bind them together, and save them. What a wonderful resource of truth for your daughter to review in the future. And maybe one day she will share those papers with her own little daughter after God's own heart.

Use mealtimes too. They present another natural opportunity to work with your daughter to color and illustrate paper place mats for the family meals (another art project!). Buy Jesus stickers and turn her loose to put them all over the mats.

Use your daughter's lunch box or backpack. Put Bible

verses about God's love for her on the napkin inside—and a sticker if you have one, along with a message of your love and prayers for her and any problems she may be having at school, in her classroom, or with friendships.

Read about the life of Jesus.

There's no better way to get to know Jesus than by reading about Him every day of your daughter's life while she's still under your roof. His life story and teachings are found in the four Gospels—Matthew, Mark, Luke, and John. Is your daughter young? Is she just learning to read? Then read out loud to her daily from one of the Gospels. As she gets older and is able to read, have her share in the Bible reading. Also have her write out and memorize key verses such as "Jesus said to him, 'I am the way, the truth, and the life. No one comes to the Father except through me'" (John 14:6).

Purpose to talk about Jesus.

This takes reading about Jesus to the next level. You want your daughter to know that Jesus is God in human flesh. And you want her to know why He came to earth. You want her to know the gospel—the good news! That means you need to vocally and repeatedly talk about the facts—the gospel facts. What is the gospel? First Corinthians 15:3-4 gives a succinct summary. "Christ died for our sins according to the Scriptures, and…He was buried, and…He rose again the third day according to the Scriptures."

Mom's Think Pad

Before you move on to your next Mom Mission, take a minute or two to think about what you can do to track with God as a mom. Make some plans of your own to take a few small steps that make a big difference.

1. Wow! Me? A preacher? Whatever You say, Lord. Now, what should my next "sermon" to my daughter be?

2. Lord, me a farmer? But I get it. I need to sow more seed. What verse can I share with my girl today, a verse that's special to me or one that will help her with a problem she's having?

3. When I think about Timothy's mom and grandmom, I want to be like them (2 Timothy 1:5; 3:15). I want my daughter to know Jesus. Here are three things I will do to follow in their steps:

4. What's the best time today—when I'm with my daughter—to tell her how I met Jesus? I'll make it an appointment!

5. Being a mom is not always fun or easy, for sure! But I don't want to give up or lose sight of the goal of raising a daughter after God's own heart. The verse I want to memorize for strength and encouragement is this (choose a verse, write it here, and hide it in your heart):

Chapter 4

The Coach

To obey is better than sacrifice...
—1 Samuel 15:22

Why is it that anything worthwhile comes with a price tag? For example, my physical body. For years I threatened to get in shape. Finally, after one more failed attempt at keeping a New Year's resolution dealing with my physical condition—and following my doctor's advice—I took a giant step and signed up for a series of sessions with a fitness trainer at the military gym where my Jim worked out. I thought, *Hey, I could just go along with Jim and meet with my new trainer. It'll be like a date!* Well, Day One, Session One arrived, and boy oh boy was I in for a big surprise when I arrived for my first workout, eager to hit the gym floor.

With my new resolve, I was ready to "pump some iron"! Instead, to my disappointment, Cleve and I spent most of the first session in the gym office assessing my general health, medications, eating habits, fluid intake, and my reasons and goals for wanting a trainer's help. It wasn't until the very end of the hour that Cleve acquainted me with the weight machines I would use... at our next session!

As time passed, Cleve added more exercises and more repetitions as my muscles adjusted to the conditioning and grew stronger. Not only was Cleve my trainer, but he also took on the role of coach and mentor in the fitness realm. He even became somewhat of a friend as, during those sessions, I learned a little about him and his wife and children.

I was thrilled! I was motivated and doing well. But Cleve kept applying more pressure for me to keep moving forward in achieving my goals. Because he was such a good trainer, both tough and understanding of my special needs, I met my goals...and more! Our sessions ended, but these eight years later, guess what? I'm still working out and doing the exercises Cleve trained me to do. And because of his faithful reminders and instruction about my diet and health, I'm still following the regimen he instilled in me.

Taking on Another Mission

Today we come to a new assignment in your mission to raise a daughter after God's own heart. We are adding the role of coach, trainer, and maybe even a dash of drill sergeant and sheriff thrown in at times. Unlike my two or three months of meeting with a trainer, you have your daughter for about 20 years. And you get to "meet" with her every day. I got great results in a brief few months, but with the massive amount of time God gives you with your daughter, you have an even greater opportunity to impress and influence and train her in every area—for life!

So welcome to God's circle of coaches of daughters! What is the objective of your time spent training your daughter? It is first and foremost to help her develop a heart that follows God, that delights in being compliant, cooperative, and responsive to Him and His will. It is to nurture in her a heart that obeys.

Unfortunately, even from an early age, the fallen human spirit wants to rebel against authority and especially against God's rules. So don't take it personally when your daughter says, "No!" as soon as she can talk. Your mission, mom, is to patiently but firmly coach her to the place where her heart's desire is to obey all types of authority. God is first on the list. But obedience to you and her dad as parents, then teachers at school, then to authority figures and rules and laws follow right behind.

Two Kinds of Hearts

If you've read any of my books with *After God's Own Heart* in the title, you know this phrase comes from the Bible—from Acts 13:22. Here God gives a description of the man David. God testified, "I have found David the son of Jesse, a man after My own heart, who will do all My will."

This commentary was in sharp contrast to the character of Saul, who was the reigning king of Israel at the time God pronounced that David was a man after His own heart. These two men had two different kinds of hearts. David had an obedient heart. He responded to the Lord God with a desire to do what was right. He yearned to follow God and do His will.

Saul, however, had a selfish heart. His obedience was merely external. He wasn't concerned with following God's will. Saul only wanted to do things his way.

God gave both of these men the same opportunity—the honor of leading God's people, the nation of Israel. But in the end they walked two different paths. David walked toward God, and Saul walked away from God.

Now let's switch from David and Saul's heart conditions to yours. Life coaching starts with you, mom, and with your heart. Your daughter needs you to model a heart that loves God and desires to follow His will. Where else is she going to see this godly trait up close and personal—and daily, if not in you? So it follows that a major step in your daughter developing a heart of obedience is seeing it modeled in you. This is the "passive training" she receives from you as you teach by your example. Now for the "active training"!

"Train Up a Child"

These are the opening words to Proverbs 22:6, which tells parents to "train up a child in the way he should go, and when he is old he will not depart from it."

As a new Christian mom at age 28 with two little girls, I first heard this verse quoted in a mom's group at my church. This sounded like a fabulous "mothering verse," so I rolled up my mothering sleeves and tried to do just as the verse instructs. Later as I began to study and eventually teach the mom's group, I wanted to get a better understanding of what it means to "train up" a child.

In the books I checked out from the church library, I learned that the verb translated "train" includes the idea of "narrowing" or "hedging in." In other words, to train means to build curbs that channel right behavior. Child-raising involves starting a child in the right direction by "narrowing" his or her conduct away from evil and toward godliness. One Bible scholar suggests that the possible meanings of "train" are to "[d]edicate the child to God. Prepare the child for his future responsibilities. Exercise or train the child for adulthood."[15]

Next, I found that "in the way he should go" means the proper way, the path of wise godly living. This path is emphasized throughout the book of Proverbs as the way of wisdom. When a parent is faithful to "train up a child in the way he should go," that child should continue in it when he or she is grown and attains adulthood. To repeat the scholar's statement, a parent is to "prepare the child for his future responsibilities." This means that in addition to helping your child grow spiritually, you are also to offer guidance regarding the physical, mental, social, and financial aspects of daily life. As you can see, mom, your coaching assignment is all laid out for you!

And where is the ideal "training facility" for preparing your daughter to ultimately become a woman after God's own heart? Your home!

To make your coaching job more simple, God gives one specific command for you to teach your daughter: She is told to "obey [her] parents in the Lord, for this is right" (Ephesians 6:1). That's it! That's why I can say that Christian coaching starts at home. If your daughter learns to carry out this one command, then she is well on her way to becoming not only a daughter after God's own heart, but someday, sooner that you think, a woman who follows God with all her heart.

Ephesians 6:1 sounds a little self-serving, doesn't it? I mean, it would be great and make mothering a dream to have your girl do whatever you ask! But God knows that if your daughter learns obedience at home, toward you and her dad, she will be obedient and submissive to God and His Word, to the laws of the land, and to authorities at school and in society.

Discipline Is a Part of Coaching

As a kid, my husband played all kinds of sports at school. He loved competing. He loved the physical exercise. And he loved being on a team and a part of something exciting. But he didn't love what happened when he failed to do what the coach wanted—when he had to run extra laps, or practice longer, or sit on the bench while others were put into the game.

Well, my fellow mom-coach, you'll have to do some disciplining as well. You'll have to put in some time correcting your daughter's behavior and enforcing family rules. You'll have to work as a partner with God—the Ultimate Coach—and follow His rules for parents as you work with Him in your girl's life. Here are some coaching guidelines for those times when things aren't going "in the way they should go." You need to...

Realize the *why* of discipline: "Foolishness is bound up in the heart of a child; the rod of correction will drive it far from him" (Proverbs 22:15).

See the upside of discipline: "Chasten your son while there is hope" (Proverbs 19:18).

Learn to discipline right away: "He who spares his rod hates his son, but he who loves him disciplines him promptly" (Proverbs 13:24).

Understand the long-range benefit of discipline: "Do not withhold correction from a child, for if you beat him with a rod, he will not die. You shall beat him with a rod, and deliver his soul from hell" (Proverbs 23:13-14).

Key in on the personal blessings of discipline: "Correct your son, and he will give you rest; Yes, he will give delight to your soul" (Proverbs 29:17).

Believe me, I know God's instruction to discipline can be hard to swallow and harder to do. And I know all the arguments and criticisms against disciplining children. Here are a few favorites we moms use for failing to discipline:

—Are you kidding? That's physical abuse!

—I can't be a part of anything that inflicts pain.

—I tried it once, and it didn't work.

—Surely there are other ways to get through to my girl!

—I'll just reason with my daughter.

—My daughter's so cute! How could I ever make her cry?

—Kids are kids! Sure, they'll act up. So what?

—My girl is basically good. She'll grow out of it. I just need to give her time.

—Discipline is barbaric and reeks of "Dark Age" thinking.

—My husband and I don't agree on how to discipline, so we don't.

—Discipline takes a lot of time, which I don't have.

—I don't like to discipline. I just want happy times.

—Discipline ruins the home atmosphere.

—I don't know how to discipline, so I don't.

—I'm afraid I'll do it wrong, so I don't do it at all.

—Confrontation is not my thing.

—I'm letting the schoolteachers deal with behavioral issues.

—I don't know if I believe in what the Bible says about child discipline.

Here's an encouraging thought: Approach the disciplining of your daughter in the same way you would the care of a rose bush. You know that if you prune, shape, and train your plant, it will experience healthy growth and bear fragrant and splendid blossoms. A gardener must cut away what is ugly and unhealthy before a rose bush can bring forth all its incredible beauty.

Do the hard thing, mom. Discipline your daughter. God intends for her to become a young woman of polished, sculptured, graceful beauty (Psalm 144:12).

Life Areas That Require a Coach

Moving on...the Bible reminds us that there is a time to tear down and a time to build up (Ecclesiastes 3:3). Let's just say that correcting your daughter is the "tearing down" of bad habits and behaviors. Then comes the fun part—the life coaching, the building up of your princess's character.

Her Spiritual Life

Once your daughter learns obedience, then the remaining areas of life will be a joy to teach. She will be a willing student as you coach her toward maturity—especially spiritual maturity. Your coaching will include showing her how to study her Bible and teaching her how to pray. As she takes your training to heart, she will become a woman of great beauty as she reflects the heart of Jesus and His fruit of the Spirit.

Once your daughter learns obedience, then the remaining areas of life will be a joy to teach.

Her Physical Life

Some girls seem to be born with an internal sense for what's prim and proper. From an early age they are neat and concerned with cleanliness. Then there are the rest of us, who need help with just about every area of our physical life! When it comes to your daughter, you get the privilege of coaching her in all areas of health—good food choices, exercise, dental hygiene, and getting her rest. She will also need your coaching when it comes to the natural changes every maturing girl faces. And she'll need you to educate her about modesty, makeup, and hairstyles. Just make sure you don't allow the world to coach your little girl! No, she needs to understand God's standards for her dress and conduct from her mom, from *you*, from a coach who loves and cares for her.

Her Financial Life

From her first allowance or the gift of a five-dollar bill tucked into a birthday card from her grandparents, your little girl comes face-to-face with the need to deal with money. Money is a necessary daily commodity your daughter must learn how to manage. Each day is an opportunity for you to teach her what the Bible says about the use of money and its proper place in her life. She'll need to learn how to earn it, save it, budget it, use it, and give it away. And you get to coach her with regard to what God says about the relationship between hard work and financial reward. So put on your coaching hat and roll up your sleeves!

Her Social Life

This book includes a chapter on your mission as "the social secretary" for your daughter. For now, though, just acknowledge that you—as her mom—can control her friendships and time with friends to some extent. And you can instruct her and guide her behavior while she is with you at home. But as time goes on, your daughter will spend less and less time with you at home. How you coach her in private now will determine how she manages herself in public later. Your goal is to instill in her heart and mind what God's Word teaches about the kinds of friends she should and should not have. Your job is to teach her proper conduct for a girl, young woman, and woman "professing godliness"—who is pursuing God with all her heart (1 Timothy 2:10).

Her Vocational Life

Each child is different. (Is this an understatement or what?!) Your daughter is her own unique person. Yes, she has some of your genetic makeup within her, but she is not you. And God does not mean for her to be viewed as an extension of your unrealized hopes and dreams. I've met many a mom who always wanted to be a cheerleader but didn't make the squad. So what does a mom like this do when a daughter comes along? She determines, "That girl is going to be a cheerleader even if it kills me...and her!"

Your job, mom, as your daughter's coach, is to introduce her to a variety of pursuits that lead to the discovery and use of her God-given abilities and talents. By encouraging her through crafts, music, languages, journaling, etc., you will help her to become aware of what she loves and where she excels. Once these aptitudes are revealed and developed, they will provide the expression and personal fulfillment of her creativity at home, at church, and in her community. Who knows? They may even lead her into a particular job or profession.

Her Mental Life

God has given your little girl a mind, and He expects that mind to function to its greatest capacity. This is where you come in, mom. You have 18-plus years to help your daughter develop her mind. This is when you get to enforce the three Rs—reading, 'riting (writing), and 'rithmetic (arithmetic).

You don't know where God will place your daughter as an adult. But you do know you need to prepare her for her future. Will she become a scientist, pharmacist, or manager and use her mind to earn degrees, do research, and lead? Will she move to a foreign country and use her mind to learn a new language? Will she marry a man who serves God on the mission field and translates the Bible, and use her mind to help with the translation work? Will she have a child with a life-threatening illness or a permanent disability and use her mind to learn the best ways to care for such a precious one? Or will she—like all homemakers—run a busy household, manage the family budget, plan and prepare meals, create a schedule, maybe even homeschool her children, and...well, you know the drill.

The ways your daughter might need to use her mind are as unlimited and unknown as her future. Your job? Coach her to enjoy learning, to do her school work, to be a reader, and to stretch her mind by exploring new subjects.

Her Family Life

You'll find an entire chapter on this most basic area of life. But for now, note that coaching your daughter to function in a family unit is key. It's for life. Sure, she's a daughter and a sister right now. But one day she'll probably be a wife and mom with her own family. Your job at this time is to teach your girl how to be a loving daughter, sister, and granddaughter. You'll be showing her the ropes when it comes to being kind and helpful to her siblings (like helping her brother find his backpack instead of ragging on him and secretly being glad he messed up). You get to train her to spoil her dad. You get to ingrain in her the courtesy of sending thank-you notes to family members who give her gifts, and the kindness of sending spontaneous cards and letters, e-mails and text messages—even phone calls!

Let her live right next to you. Let her see with her own eyes and hear with her own ears how thoughtful you are. How you love to be helpful and kind at home. How you never bat an eye at going the extra mile in serving the family with a cheerful, giving heart.

Her Church Life

I cannot say this enough: Church is essential in raising a daughter after God's own heart. So you, mom, the church lady, have the awesome opportunity to coach your daughter in the importance of church attendance, involvement, and ministry.

How is this best done? First of all, start early! Help her develop a heart that is merciful and kind and wants to help people. Then let her watch you and be with you at church. Let her follow you around as you minister to others. Let her assist you as you serve in any way. Imagine the church that has *two* of *you* because you were faithful to pass on your love for the church to your daughter!

A Word of Encouragement

God has given you the stewardship of raising your daughter to follow Him, to train her up in the way she should go. And He's given you everything you need for the job: His principles and instructions right out of His Word. His wisdom when you ask for it (James 1:5). His fruit of the Spirit—love, patience, and self-control—when you need it (Galatians 5:22-23). The avenue of prayer, your direct link to Him—when you use it. Mentors in the body of Christ—who can guide you. As a favorite scripture of mine tells us, "His divine power has given to us all things that pertain to life and godliness" (2 Peter 1:3).

You Can Do It!

Each of the following suggestions is something you can do to contribute toward becoming the mom you dream of being. And each one betters your life...and your daughter's too. Here we go:

Start with the basics.

It's never too early to start preparing your daughter, and it's certainly never too late to begin training in the basic areas of her life. The spiritual area is obvious and key. But the mental, physical, social, financial, and vocational areas are all part of your daughter's daily existence. And it's true that if you are starting when she's older, the challenges—and maybe even the resistance—may be greater. But with your faithful persistence and a heart full of love, the blessings will be great too! In your prayer notebook or maybe a "My Daughter's Heart" book, make headings for each area of life in which life coaching is needed, and start writing down goals and ideas to work on with your daughter.

Get the help you need.

Maybe you're like I was and don't have a clue about being a Christian mom. What can you do? Sign up for a parenting class. There you'll learn biblical principles about raising up children—principles that last a lifetime. These guidelines from Scripture will stand the test of time and will help you show your daughter what God says about every practical area of life. And you can always read a book. In fact, read lots of books! Read a little something every day just to keep you on your toes as you raise your daughter from toddling times to teen times. Don't miss out on the wisdom books can offer you.

Follow the good example of others.

Think of a mom you admire. Then describe her. What is it you like or see in her that you want to copy? And think about parents who seem to have their act together in the parenting department. Start observing the ways they deal with their children. Then do what my husband and I did. When we had an issue with our girls in their teen years, we went to four couples and asked their advice. Their responses were encouraging, helpful, specific, and gave us direction. Many have already walked the road you are on right now. Watch, look, listen, and write down what they have to say. Then put those lessons to work!

Keep adjusting.

Things change. You change. Your daughter changes. The makeup of the family changes. And there are other kinds of changes—moving to another state, taking on a different job. Through it all, hopefully you are changing into a more Christlike woman and mom. So regularly review and adjust your child-raising strategies. Constantly evaluate your training and methods of discipline. What's working? What's not? Pray, and don't be afraid—or too proud—to seek advice if things aren't working. There's plenty of help out there—just ask! What adjustments do you need to make today?

Enjoy the ride.

Being a mom is a big job, a 24/7 job! But it can and should be a fun job. Training takes time, effort, and planning, but that doesn't mean you and your daughter can't have lots of fun along the way. Be silly once in a while. Plan some crazy outings. Go on a trip together. Take your teen daughter with you to the women's retreat. As her coach, plan for fun.

Mom's Think Pad

Before you move on to your next Mom Mission, take a minute or two to think about what you can do to track with God as a mom. Make some plans of your own to take a few small steps that make a big difference.

1. I used to be on a team or a member of a group. What are some things my coach or leader did that really helped me? Encouraged me? Brought out the best in me?

2. What did I do yesterday to coach, instruct, and train my daughter? A better question is this: What will I do tomorrow to be her hands-on life coach?

3. Lord, help me to set one weekly goal for my girl in each of these areas of her precious life:

   Spiritual—

   Physical—

   Social—

   Vocational—

Mental—

Family—

Church—

4. I'm thinking about what it means to "train" my daughter. What curbs do I need to build for her behavior?

5. Lord, it's hard, but I accept that You want me to actively discipline and train my daughter. Help me to do this one day at a time. Help me to take this one step tomorrow:

Chapter 5

The Church Lady

Let the little children come to Me,
and do not forbid them;
for of such is the kingdom of God.
—MARK 10:14

It was Friday night. Jim and I had just spent two great hours together at a nearby fast-food restaurant. It was our "date night"—the night when our young teen girls went to their weekly youth Bible study. We had solved all the world's problems and even a few of our own, so we were feeling pretty good as we drove into the church parking lot to pick the girls up. But what we were about to experience became a story that's been repeated down through the years when we get together as a family.

When we pulled up to the gym, the study had just ended. Kids were streaming out to meet their parents. Our junior high girls spotted us, came over to the car, and excitedly hopped into the back seat. They both started talking at once—so much so that we couldn't understand what they were saying. We only caught bits and pieces here and there: "Gross?" "A tongue?" "A cow's tongue?" "Passed around the room?" "Everybody had to touch it?"

Finally we got them to settle down long enough to relate what had happened that night at youth group. Their leader had gone to the grocery store and bought a cow's tongue, which he passed around the room, making sure each teen not only looked at it, but also touched it! Then he dove into his talk about how awful it is for us to use our tongues to hurt people through gossip and hateful words.

As I said, that evening made a huge impression on our girls—and on Jim and me! Down through the years, every time the subject of gossip, slander, or mean speech was discussed in our home, that awful cow tongue was brought up right away. Even today, we all still talk about that repulsive tongue, some 25-plus years later!

The Importance of Church for My Family

My fellow mom, there isn't space to share with you all that going to church and getting our girls to church has meant to us as a family. When we became a Christian family my daughters were small, and it was easy and fun for them to go to church. By the time they grew older, going to church had become a natural and routine part of our week. We were all excited about church! We made sure Katherine and Courtney were at every children's and youth function that came around. And we went to the church work days as a family as well. We didn't have a lot of money, but we made it a priority to save for the girls' winter camp and summer camp registration fees.

Jim and I wanted Katherine and Courtney to experience Jesus in as many contexts as possible. If there was a Friday night youth event, one or both of us would take them there and then pick them up afterward at a bowling alley or skate rink or the youth pastor's home. And sometimes it was pretty late too. But it was a small sacrifice for what we hoped and prayed would plant seeds for reaping eternal dividends.

And what happened? In time, by God's grace—and maybe due a little to our example and commitment of time and effort—our wee ones grew and matured and became believers in Christ. And today, several decades later, they are now taking their little ones to church, who are learning to love Jesus and His Word, and enjoying the friends they make and the fellowship they experience at their churches.

The Time Is Now

I don't know what stage of daughter-raising you are in right now, but it's never too early to take your daughter to church. (Mary took Jesus to "church" when He was only eight days old. We see Him in the temple again at age 12—see Luke 2:21,41-46.) And it's never too late to take your daughter to church. The more she goes, the more friends she will make, and the more she will feel like she fits in, and the more fun she will have. And of course, the more steady and powerful the influence of the Word of God will have on her heart and mind.

You may be reading this and thinking, *I've tried taking my daughter to church, but she doesn't want to go. So I haven't pressed the issue, especially since I haven't been all that faithful myself. And now she's older and could care less about spiritual things.* Well, mom, hang in there. The time is now. Start praying. And start being faithful about attending church yourself.

As a parent who is responsible to train up your daughter in the things of the Lord, you already understand the importance of church. And hopefully you've been faithfully taking your daughter to church. But maybe you are a new believer (like I was) or until now you didn't realize the importance of church. For you the time is now. Start being the church lady, and start going to church.

Or maybe your daughter isn't where you are in her faith and understanding of the things of God. That's okay too. Don't let her spiritual condition deter you. Don't back down or back out. Again, the time is now. Put on your church lady mentality and make the decision to go to church, and hold to that decision. And don't forget to make going to church special—pick up donuts on the way, or have lunch out afterward. Encourage your daughter to bring along a friend. Be sure to include lots of love and encouragement...and prayer that God will break through to her heart and show her the joy of knowing the Lord.

Jesus Loves the Little Children

These words begin a favorite song our girls sang at church and at home. It also reminds me of one scene in the Bible that is very touching and gives great insight into Jesus' love for children. Here's the scene as described in Mark 10:13-16. After you read this tender story, note the different characters, their responses, and the lessons to you as a mom.

They [parents] brought little children to Him, that He might touch them; but the disciples rebuked those who brought them. But when Jesus saw it, He was greatly displeased and said to them, "Let the little children come to Me, and do not forbid them; for of such is the kingdom of God. Assuredly, I say to you, whoever does not receive the kingdom of God as a little child will by no means enter it." And He took them up in His arms, laid His hands on them, and blessed them.

The parents...made an effort to bring their children to Jesus. They were doing the right thing. They had right priorities and thought it was important to introduce and expose their little ones to Jesus. (Lesson: These parents are positive models for you to follow.)

The disciples...were trying to protect Jesus from the crowds and annoying interruptions. In their minds these children were not important and fell into the category of an unwelcome interruption. *Surely,* they may have thought, *these children are too young to receive truth from the Master!* (Lesson: Don't use this common excuse for not teaching biblical truth to your little ones or for not taking them to church.)

Jesus...took advantage of this occasion to demonstrate two truths: First, He used these young children as an illustration to both parents and the disciples, as well as to us today, that the kingdom of God must be received with childlike faith. And second, He demonstrated the special relationship He wants to have with children. He touched them, held them, and blessed them (verse 16). (Lesson: This is a scene that Jesus would want repeated through you with your daughter as well.)

How dedicated are you to bringing your daughter into the presence of Jesus? Do you read His stories and teachings from the Bible at home? And how committed are you to being the church lady? Do you faithfully take her to church? Only the grace of God can save a child, but here is some food for thought about making sure your daughter is exposed to Jesus at a young age and on a regular basis: "People are much more likely to accept Christ as their Savior when they are young. Absorption of biblical information and principles typically peaks during the preteen years."[16]

The Place of Worship

You might be wondering, *Why is going to "church" and "the church" so important? What's the big deal? Can't we worship Jesus anywhere and anytime?* Good questions! And the Bible shows us why. With the coming of God in human flesh, Jesus announced that God is spirit and as spirit, He can be worshiped anywhere and at any time (see John 4:23-24). Does this mean that you and your family can worship God at home or while you are camping in the woods? Yes!

But that doesn't answer the question as to why Jesus Himself instituted a gathering of believers which He called "My church" (Matthew 16:18). In the original Greek text of the New Testament, the word translated "church" in English comes from a term that means "called out ones." These "called out ones" met together and became the visible "body of Christ" after Jesus returned to heaven. The custom of gathering together as a body of believers has been duplicated down through the centuries. In fact, the writer of the book of Hebrews encouraged his readers and all believers through time to continue this pattern of regular group worship:

> Let us consider one another in order to stir up love and good works, not forsaking the assembling of ourselves together, as is the manner of some, but exhorting one another, and so much the more as you see the Day approaching (Hebrews 10:24-25).

At church, Christians have the opportunity to worship God together and to meet for the purpose of building up one another. It is vital for your daughter to be part of this gathering where mutual faith in Christ is shared, where she can be strengthened by others. And it is extremely important for her to know that you see this experience as a top priority. You as the church lady need to take your daughter to church with the right attitude and for the right purposes.

Unfortunately, some people think that merely being physically present at church fulfills an obligation to God. The problem with this kind of thinking is that simply showing up doesn't automatically qualify as worship. Going to church was never meant to be just a

Most little ones love *and look forward to their church group experiences. So do your part, and then trust in the Lord.*

thing you do on Sunday. And it's not to be done because it is the socially accepted Sunday morning activity, because it is the thing that's expected of you and your family. No, going to church is to be a sacrifice of worship. It's a place and an opportunity to focus on God and His Son and to learn more about them through the preaching and teaching of the Word.

Reasons Moms Don't Get Their Daughters to Church

Through the years I've mentored hundreds of moms. The first matter of business for our meetings was helping each mom establish a personal relationship with Christ. Second was to ensure that she set up a schedule that included time in God's Word each day. And third on my must-do list was making sure Mom and her children were going to church—that each mom became a church lady. As you can imagine, I've heard a lot of excuses, and here's a short list. Maybe you'll find yourself here. And, if it helps, I've personally thought of all these reasons myself at one time or another.

"Church isn't all that important." When church isn't seen as unique and essential to the spiritual growth and maturity of your daughter, it becomes like any other activity, like soccer practice or a Sunday game in a local sports league.

"Sunday is the only day we have to be together as a family at home. We go in all directions all week long, so we try to spend quality time together on Sunday." Perhaps that is true about your schedule. But church together makes Christ the glue that holds and strengthens family bonds. Take your kids to church. Don't deprive them of the excitement they can receive from the things of God. Let them be a part of something alive, spiritually alive! Then hang out together during the afternoon as a family.

"I work on Sundays. I don't know anyone who can take my daughter to church." Maybe there's nothing you can do about the fact you work on Sunday. But could you go Sunday night? Going

to church somewhere at some time on some day or night of the week is a must. That's where you and your daughter and family will enjoy exposure to Jesus. That's where spiritual growth will occur. Make going to church a priority, and make it happen, even if it means going on a weeknight.

"My daughter doesn't like the youth group. She feels like she doesn't belong." Don't let these kinds of reasons cause you to not take your daughter to church. Challenge your daughter to give the group a chance by attending at least four times. Or let her bring a friend or two. Or maybe you can help be a part of the leadership of the youth group.

"I'm afraid to leave my daughter with a group of kids. She might get sick." Yes, she might. All kids get sick sooner or later. But you have every right to ask those in charge of the nursery or classroom what health precautions are being taken. Most churches are serious about sanitizing every item in the nurseries and children's classrooms each week. And most little ones *love* and look forward to their church group experiences. So do your part, and then trust the Lord.

"My toddler cries and acts up. She doesn't want me to leave her in her classroom. It's just too much of a hassle." What you don't always know is that most children stop crying and struggling and start playing as soon as Mom disappears around the corner. Be strong and be firm. Realize this is important training because, Lord willing, your daughter will be going to church the rest of her life.

"My daughter already goes to a Christian school. I don't want religion to be 24/7 in her life. She needs some free time away from church stuff." Christian school is a wonderful experience, but it is not commanded in the Bible, and it's not church. At a Christian school, your daughter will receive an education. By contrast, at church, she will have the opportunity to worship God, learn from His Word, and be spiritually encouraged by other Christian kids.

Reasons Church Is So Important

How about this? Instead of focusing on reasons for not taking our daughters to church, we should focus on why church is so key—why it is vital that we be church ladies.

Church is a place where you and your daughter will hear the teaching of God's Word. What wonderful things you will have to share with each other afterward! Why? Because you were there together.

Church is a place where you and your daughter will have the opportunity to serve others. What a blessing—and how fun!—it is to work side by side as a team to help those in need, to serve a meal, and to prepare the church for its activities or clean up afterward.

Church is a place where your daughter will meet and make friends with other Christian kids and young people. Those associations will strengthen and sustain your daughter as she lives in a world of unbelief and evil outside the church. When you take her to church, you are actually giving her this gift.

Church attendance models what's important in your life. It shouts out your love for God and His Number One priority position in your heart.

You Can Do It!

Each of the following suggestions is something you can do to contribute toward becoming the mom you dream of being. And each one betters your life...and your daughter's too. Here we go:

Talk about church.

What's important to you? Whatever it is, that's what you talk about. Another way to ring your bell as the bell sheep is to talk about the joys and importance of church. It's as simple as bringing up a point from the pastor's sermon. Or maybe even sharing the joke he told. Or saying, "Oh, honey! Remember your church lesson? 'Do to others as you would want them do to you'? Let's roll Mr. White's trash can in off the street for him." Or, "Katie, let's take some of these fresh cookies to the family next door whose dad is in Iraq for a year." And you can always be on an exciting countdown: "Hey, Taylor, it's only two days until church...or your youth meeting...or Pioneer Girls... or Awana...or church camp!" Whatever it is that the church is offering, help your daughter get excited about it.

Begin the night before.

If you have been talking about church all week, it's easy to guard the evening before church. Help your daughter select and lay out her church clothes and her Bible. Set an early curfew for your daughter if she's a teen. By preparing the night before, the next morning won't be so stressful for everyone. Everyone's hearts and attitudes will be prepared for the blessings they will receive at church.

Get the most out of church.

God has given you and your daughter a tremendous resource in your church. It's a spiritual resource, a social resource, an educational resource, and a recreational resource all rolled into one. So be sure to take advantage of it. Most churches have both a service and Bible classes for adults, youth, and children. Make the effort to stay for both teaching times. If your daughter is old enough, have her sit with you in the service. Then the next hour, if there is a children's program or youth group, split your family up into the different classes to get further training in the Bible and to form friendships. Everyone gets a heavenly injection that can help sustain them until their next exposure to church.

Consider joining a Bible study.

By now you know how important your church and church involvement is, not only to your daughter, but also to you! As the bell sheep for your girl and the church lady for your family, set a goal to join a women's Bible study or a family or neighborhood group. If something is good, then more is even better. Your spiritual growth will astound you, and your devotion to the Lord will burn hotter and brighter as you grow in your knowledge of the truths of the Bible. And you'll enjoy rich fellowship, make close friends, and get involved in lives of others.

Revisit the reasons moms don't take their daughters to church.

Do any of them fit you at this time? Pause, pray, and reflect. Then be the church lady. Grab your calendar and write *church* on each Sunday and whatever other days there are studies or activities for you and your daughter. Think about any "little excuses" you have been making. Skipping church for now may seem inconsequential or unimportant, but it can have lasting effects on you and your family. Pause, pray, and reflect. Then read on to see how one excuse a mom made turned into "Generations of Excuses."

Generations of Excuses

BY MARY LOUISE KITSEN[17]

Dear Joan,

What a beautiful baby boy Ben and I have been blessed with! I cannot begin to tell you the joy he has brought to us.

You asked how Mrs. Miller is doing in church since her accident. They tell me she manages her wheelchair with amazing ease. She's still teaching Sunday school too. To tell you the truth, Ben and I haven't been to church since Timmy was born. It's just so difficult with a new baby. And I worry that he'll catch something. So many people have colds right now. When Timmy is just a little bigger, it will be so much easier.

Love, Sarah

Dear Joan,

Can you believe our Timmy is a year old already? He's so healthy and active—just beautiful.

No, we haven't really started attending church regularly yet. Timmy cried so hard when I tried to leave him in the nursery that I just could not do it. But he was just too noisy and active in church with us so we finally left early. The pastor came to visit. He assured us Timmy would be fine once we left him at the nursery, but I'm just not ready to force it yet. When he's just a little bigger, it will be so much easier.

Love, Sarah

Dear Joan,

However do you cope with three lively children? Timmy is into everything. I simply cannot control him.

We still aren't attending church regularly. I tried leaving Timmy in the nursery a few Sundays back, but he didn't get along well with the other children. The next week we took him into church with us, but he was all over the church. He'd be out of our pew before I could stop him. Several of the members sitting nearby were annoyed, but after all, Timmy's only three. It will be easier when he's just a little bit bigger.

Love, Sarah

Dear Joan,

I must be a perfectly dreadful mother! But Ben and I cannot keep our little boy under control. Last week he slipped out of our booth at a restaurant and caused a waitress to drop an entire tray of food. And last Sunday he slid out of our pew at church, and before I knew what was happening, guess where he was—right up front with the pastor! I could have fainted from embarrassment.

The pastor thinks a few hours at a preschool would be good for Timmy, but he's just four. He'll quiet down when he gets a little older.

Love, Sarah

Dear Joan,

It seems so funny to see our little boy walking off to school each morning. I thought starting him in school would be an ordeal, but Mrs. Foster must have a way with children. He seems happy as a lark.

No, Joan, we haven't started Timmy in Sunday school yet. It's just that his sister is still a new baby. And you know how hard it is getting ready to go to church with a new baby. When Sally is just a little older, it will be easier.

Love, Sarah

Dear Joan,

How the years fly by. Tim is in the fifth grade now, and little Sally just started kindergarten.

No, I'm afraid we aren't as faithful about attending Sunday school and church as we should be. With work for Ben and the children in school, we just don't get a chance to be together much during the week. And on Saturday there are always so many errands to run. Sunday is really the best time to spend some time together, and we like to start early. Last Sunday we drove to Lake Manaware. It's quite a distance. You really cannot wait until after church. These years are so special.

Love, Sarah

Dear Joan,

Teenagers certainly have a mind of their own! I simply cannot get Tim to attend Sunday school and church at all. He doesn't even want to go to youth fellowship. He thinks their activities are "dumb." He isn't getting along as well in school as Ben and I would like either. He doesn't seems to get along with his teachers or the other students. I wish we lived in a different town. There just seems to be something missing in this one.

Sally? She goes to Sunday school sometimes, but you know how little ones are. She thinks everything her brother does or thinks is perfect. But after all, the teen years are so difficult. It's a time of adjustment. When Tim matures a little more, he'll see things differently, and then his adoring little sister will too.

Love, Sarah

Dear Joan,

How I wish you and Tom could have made the wedding. It was so very beautiful. Tim looked so handsome, and his bride was just a vision. The church was filled, and everything was so lovely.

No, Tim and his bride haven't started attending church regularly yet. But after all, they are newlyweds. They enjoy just being together. So young and so in love. But they'll settle down in a little while, and then church will become a part of their lives.

Love, Sarah

Dear Joan,

Ben and I are grandparents! Tim and his Margie have the most darling baby boy you could ever hope to see. We are all so proud of him.

Church? Well, Ben and I just don't seem to go as often as we should. Ben's been promoted at the office again, and he sometimes plays golf with his boss on Sunday morning. And Sally is a teen now, and she's got her own interests. When things change, we'll get to church more often.

Tim and Margie? Oh, they can't really manage church right now. You know how hard it is with a new baby. And I warned Margie about letting the baby get exposed to colds that seem to be going around right now. When the baby is a little bigger, it will be easier. I'm sure they'll become active in church. After all, Tim was raised in a Christian home by Christian parents...He has a good example to follow...

Love, Sarah

Mom's Think Pad

Before you move on to your next Mom Mission, take a minute or two to think about what you can do to track with God as a mom. Make some plans of your own to take a few small steps that can make a big difference.

1. What are my childhood memories of going to church? Hmmm—here are a few:

2. I know being a church lady who gets her kids to church is important. Here are some steps I will begin taking today to get us to church this week:

3. When I think about what Jesus said about the value of bringing children—my children!—to Him in Mark 10:13-16, how do I relate to

—the parents?

—the disciples?

—Jesus' message?

What changes in actions and attitude do I need to make?

4. Wow, that list of excuses for missing church hit me hard!
   I have to admit that sometimes my favorite excuse is
   this one:

   "Lord, help me with my own weak areas. Give me a
   heart that yearns to be with Your people and to share
   that experience with my daughter. Help me be faithful.
   Amen."

Chapter 6

The Social Secretary

He who walks with wise men will be wise.
—PROVERBS 13:20

For 30-plus years Jim and I and our daughters lived in Los Angeles County. I think the latest population statistic for that county is more than nine million, and I'm not sure how many millions live in the adjacent counties crammed with more people who commute to work in LA County. As a family we've put in what feels like half a lifetime in hours on freeways. And we've done our share of fast-lane bumper-to-bumper high-speed driving. We lived large—as in large schools, large malls, large churches, large venues. You name it, it's *large* in LA!

But about ten years ago, after our nest was empty, Jim and I moved to what we call "our little cabin in the woods" on the spectacularly breathtaking and beautiful Olympic Peninsula in the state of Washington. It was quite a change, going from city to country. From a mega-metropolis to a tiny town. From a tract home with cement-block walls between dwellings to a split-level home with a panoramic view of miles of forest and snowcapped Mount Rainier. From being two of eight million residents in Los Angeles to the Hood Canal off the Puget Sound with three neighbors on nearby properties in a rural paradise filled with fir, pine, and cedar trees. I have to say, for us it has been a marvelous change. We found the peace and quiet that's perfect for us as writers.

One of the side benefits we hadn't anticipated is the wildlife that lives here too. We are not alone! Each day presents a steady parade of animals and an air show of feathered friends, each creature with a story to tell and lessons to teach—especially to you and me as mothers who have children.

I'm sure you've heard fascinating stories and seen thrilling video footage of mother bears, lions, eagles, and—well, mothers of *all* species—protecting and training their offspring. They are fierce. They are defensive. They are vigilant. They are instructive. And they are thorough. Jim and I have witnessed these animal traits firsthand. Although there are no lions in the area (mountain lions, for sure, but thank goodness no African lions!), we see eagles daily and we've observed bears from a distance. No matter what the species, these moms all share the same goal for their young ones—survival.

Lessons Learned from God's Creatures

Well, get ready to join the animal kingdom's circle of moms! Like a lioness, a mother eagle, and a she-bear, your goal as a mom is your daughter's survival and well-being.

I don't know about you and your daughter, but when it came to anyone who had the potential to hurt our daughters in some way or other, my claws and fangs came out! When my girls were preschoolers, I wanted them to be safe as they played together in the yard or with other children, as they crossed the street, or when they visited a neighbor's house. I made it my business to know every neighbor and every kid on the block.

I also made our home a place for all the kids to come and play. When the gang was in our home, I was able to set the rules and monitor behavior. And if the kids were all playing in our yard, I could see and hear what was going on and call to my girls to come in at any time. I knew firsthand what my girls were doing and the character of our little visitors and the sort of potential influence they might have on my little darlings.

As time went by and we made friends with all our neighbors, we began to invite the kids who were in my daughters' age bracket to go with us to church and to church activities for kids. At one time we were wagging nine boys and girls to church and Awana Cubbies and Sparks on a regular basis! When it came to our neighborhood, our goal was not separation from others. No, not at all. It was to befriend these dear people and do as Jesus said—to be salt and light (Matthew 5:13-14). We had tons of fun with swimming parties, birthday parties, pancake breakfasts, skating outings, and church ventures. Our aim was to be a social center of sorts for all kids—and the social secretary for our girls.

Then off to school Katherine and Courtney went! Well, obviously I couldn't stay with them 24/7, day and night. But I drove them to school and picked them up afterward. I tried to arrive early before the final bell and took time to talk with and get to know as many parents as possible.

Then, as the social secretary, I began inviting our girls' new friends over to the house for kind of a play date. I made it a point to always make arrangements with their friends' moms and to be very specific about exactly where the girls would be and what they would be doing. I gave other moms a precise time line, and I made it clear that I would be present with the kids every minute. It was good for my daughters to spend time with other girls. (You know the scene!) In the early years, it was dolls and costumes. And as their ages progressed, so did their activities. But it was usually at our house and for short periods of time—a few hours of fun and friends.

In case you're thinking, *I can't believe this mom checked out everyone before she let her girls spend time with them,* here's what happened to me. Somewhere on this planet there was another mom who was "the *ultimate* social secretary." She knew that her daughter and one of mine had become close friends at church. So she called and invited Katherine over. Then she said she wanted to come pick up Katherine at our house, and asked if I could I please allow about ten minutes for her to visit a bit with me.

We had a nice chat, and believe me, I knew I was being checked out. I generally keep a tidy house (and with two kids, I'm sure you know that doesn't mean 100 percent tidy or spotless!). But based on how our home sweet home looked that day, this caring mom could see for herself that there was more order than chaos under our roof. (Whew!) No way was her daughter going to come to my house in the future until Mom had seen it and knew exactly where she would be leaving her daughter and the environment she would be in.

Well, later that day when I went to pick Katherine up at *her* home, I did what I had just learned from this mom extraordinaire—I checked out her residence!

My point is not to be snooty or judgmental. Just be friendly... and be aware. Be cautious. Be careful. Is the place where your daughter might possibly visit a healthy environment for her? Do things seem all right? And do relationships within the household seem positive and wholesome? Use your "mom radar" to determine what's best for your daughter. She doesn't have to be friends with every girl. And she doesn't need to spend time in the homes of all the girls she meets. We are talking about protecting your daughter. You, mom, are in charge of her social calendar—and you will be for about 20 years! The younger your daughter is, the more in charge you are. To repeat, she can and should be friendly to everyone, but she doesn't have to be friends with everyone.

Lessons Learned from Seasoned Moms

I'm so thankful for the older women and seasoned moms God gave to me as guides when I needed help. They taught me several fundamental rules to raise a daughter by. Here are two:

Don't Rush Things

The goal is to thoroughly enjoy each and every age and stage your sweet girl goes through. To get the most out of each passage. To bond and strengthen your ties with each other. To help her develop the skills and behaviors that contribute to her maturity.

The message from these wise women to me was this: Don't be in a hurry for your child to grow up, or get through her "terrible twos" or her "traumatic teens" (which are both actually quite terrific!) or whatever level of development she's in. There's nothing wrong with keeping your little one right there close with you at home, under the shadow of your wings. She doesn't need to rush into social get-togethers. She doesn't need a lot of play dates. And as the years pass, she doesn't need regular sleepovers or dates. Just let her be a sweet little mommy's girl for as long as she would like to be.

Each passage your daughter goes through is important. We already know how much a baby girl wants only Mommy and no one else! And six-year-olds love their mom to pieces and love being with her. Ten-year-olds crave an outing and time with mom—especially if it includes shopping for crafts or clothes... and food!

Be Careful

The Bible is very clear about what kinds of people are to be in—and out of—our children's lives.

Be extremely careful when it comes to the people in your daughter's world. The Bible leaves no doubt about what kinds of people are to be in—and out of—our children's lives. God wants to protect His children—and yours—from harm, evil, trouble, and costly consequences. To do this He gave us His Word, His wisdom, His instruction, His guidelines. Therefore God has quite a list of dos and don'ts to guide you as you guide your daughter. And He enlists your help as possibly the most important person in her life—you, her mom!

As I spent time with mentors, I came to the point where I had to own the fact that my job was to know these guidelines and receive them as God's standards. I had to realize I needed to enforce them. And make the choices for my daughters when they were young and growing up, as well as teach them to my girls so they, in turn, could follow them on their own.

God's Guidelines for Friends and Friendships

As a mom, do you ever wonder what's right and what's wrong? What's vital and what's not so important? What are the few choices that make all the difference? Well, when it comes to your daughter, God takes away all the wondering and tells you point blank exactly what's essential when it comes to friends and friendships.

The Wrong Kinds of Friends

When your daughter is old enough to start learning about how to pick the right kinds of friends, take some time to talk with her about the criteria God lists in His Word. As the two of you read through the following verses together, note the speech, character, and conduct of those who are most definitely *not* to be your daughter's friends. In short, help her see that God tells her to beware of any person who is...

> *A fool*—"He who walks with wise men will be wise, but the companion of fools will be destroyed" (Proverbs 13:20).
>
> *Violent*—"A violent man entices his neighbor [or friend], and leads him in a way that is not good" (Proverbs 16:29).
>
> *Hot-tempered and angry*—"Make no friendship with an angry [person], and with a furious [person] do not go" (Proverbs 22:24). God even tells you why this is important for your daughter: "Lest [she] learn his ways and set a snare for [her] soul" (verse 25).
>
> *A gossip*—"A man who flatters his neighbor spreads a net for his feet" (Proverbs 29:5).
>
> *Evil*—"Do not be deceived: Evil company corrupts good habits" (1 Corinthians 15:33).
>
> *Immoral*—"I have written to you not to keep company with anyone...who is sexually immoral, or covetous, or an idolater, or a reviler, or a drunkard, or an extortioner—not even to eat with such a person" (1 Corinthians 5:11).

The Right Kinds of Friends

Now here's a much more pleasant list to share with your daughter. God cares for her, and He wants to protect her from those who would harm her or influence her away from Him and toward evil. So He provided these scriptures to help her find the right kinds of friends.

Wise—"He who walks with wise men will be wise, but the companion of fools will be destroyed" (Proverbs 13:20).

Faithful—"A man who has friends must himself be friendly, but there is a friend who sticks closer than a brother" (Proverbs 18:24).

Honest—"Faithful are the wounds of a friend, but the kisses of an enemy are deceitful" (Proverbs 27:6).

A Christian—"Do not be unequally yoked together with unbelievers. For what fellowship has righteousness with lawlessness? And what communion has light with darkness? And what accord has Christ with Belial? Or what part has a believer with an unbeliever?" (2 Corinthians 6:14-15).

Who Are the People in Your Daughter's Life?

As a mom, you will probably have to go through a few "battles" that revolve around your daughter's friends and friendships as your little girl gets older. But it's important to remember that God has made *you* the mom. He's entrusted your daughter to *you*. He's assigned *you* to raise her "in the training and admonition of the Lord" (Ephesians 6:4), to "train" her up in the way she should go (Proverbs 22:6). And He expects you to live out your role, even when you're not too popular with your very own daughter.

But come what may, no matter what response you are getting, you must keep on teaching and instructing her from God's Word. Then the attitude or conduct you are advocating and enforcing reflects *God's* standard, not just yours.

My point is this: No matter what your daughter's age is, whether she's an infant or an 18-year-old princess, *be* a mom. Be *her* mom, and be a mom who's following Jesus. Care! Like the hen-eagle, the lioness, and the she-bear, be fierce and attentive. Be right there by your girl's side as much as possible and all the way. Instruct her. Don't leave her without help. Watch over her. Protect her—not just physically, but in every way, especially when it comes to the people in her life.

Friends and friendships are an important part of your daughter's life. Friends are part of God's plan and a major means of mutual growth, encouragement, excitement, learning, and love, along with opportunities for witnessing and evangelism. And biblical friendships definitely are a blessing to us, and to our daughters as well. So an important part of being your daughter's social secretary is monitoring social contacts and teaching her how to choose the right kinds of friends.

Three Kinds of People

One bit of wisdom you need to share with your daughter at the right age is that there are three types of people she will meet:

—Those who will pull her down.

—Those who will pull her along.

—Those who will pull her up.

Pray that God will protect her from the first category and lead her to the final two kinds of friends.

Choosing the Right Kinds of Friendships

Christian friends—Based on God's guidelines for friends, encourage your daughter to choose Christians as her *best friends*. These kids are usually found at church. And usually they are the ones who will either pull your daughter along and even up in her journey toward spiritual maturity. As we saw in "The Church Lady" chapter, one of your key roles as a mom after God's own heart is to get your daughter to church. Think about it: Generally at church there is no bad language, no arguing, no raised voices, no fighting. The kids there usually come from homes and families that live by Christian standards. And most of the people at church are there because they know God and want to know Him better.

Non-Christian friends—It is important to protect your daughter and to teach her to be wise when it comes to finding friends. But you can't keep her totally sheltered from being in contact with others, especially if she goes to public school. Don't make her afraid of life and people who are not Christians. Rather, show her it's good to be friendly to all and have friends at school and in the neighborhood. After all, wasn't Jesus "a friend of...sinners" (Luke 7:34)?

Boyfriends—For most moms, the day their daughters reach dating age (whatever that is) is a most dreaded day. Why? Because of all that's associated with dating, especially boys! If or when you choose to let your daughter date or court, here are a few start-up principles: The young man she goes out with *must* be a Christian. God's Word is 100 percent clear on this (2 Corinthians 6:14). This is His Rule #1. Beyond this #1 absolute, her date should be someone you know or have met and spent time with. And it's a good idea to limit dating to group outings, and to keep the length of the date to two or so hours in length. You will find your way on the issue of boyfriends, but these few guidelines will help get you started in the right direction.

A Concise Job Description

Now let's wrap up this vital mission assignment of social secretary. As a mom, the parent of your daughter, lay out your standards. Communicate them to her. And hold to them. Having standards will protect your daughter from dealing with unnecessary and premature emotions, from peer pressure, and from the wrong kinds of girl and boyfriends

And, as my older and more experienced mentor moms told me: Don't rush things! Be careful! And I would add, be prayerful!

You Can Do It!

Each of the following suggestions is something you can do to contribute toward becoming the mom you dream of being. And each one betters your life...and your daughter's too. Here we go:

Know where your daughter is at all times.

Have you heard the TV or radio slogan that announces, "It's ten p.m. Do you know where your children are?" A mom who's a faithful social secretary and guard dog par excellence would be able to answer this question. That's because she knows all, sees all, and is in all places at all times. We have a neighbor whose mother is married to a retired Army general. Patricia's mom comes to visit and likes to bring her little granddaughter to play outside. While they are out in the yard, she stands with her arms folded and watches over that little girl like a hawk! It's like she has eyes in the back of her head. She's like the Proverbs 31 woman, who "watches over the ways of her household"—and her granddaughter (verse 27). Believe me, I took her example to heart and made it my practice. This loving vigilance must never cease. As your daughter grows older, your watch-care becomes even more important.

Get to know your daughter's friends.

The best way to get to know the girls your daughter spends time with is to invite them to your home for snacks and fun. While they're there, try to get to know each girl. Don't turn the encounter into an FBI interrogation session. Just catch a sense of the character and depth of maturity of your daughter's friends. Notice their strong (or weak) qualities. Step into your daughter's world, and let her friends step into yours. It's a blessing for them to be in your home.

Monitor your daughter's outings.

The day will come when another girl invites your daughter to a sleepover or a trip to the mall. She may also be asking a half-dozen other girls to spend the night at her house. All I can say is to repeat what my older women told me: "Don't be in a hurry. Be careful!" This is a big step. Consider that a sleepover may last for as long as 18 hours, which is a lot of time for little or big girls to fill up in positive, edifying ways. Who will be there? And what adults and older kids will be there? What are the planned activities? Will they watch DVDs? If so, which ones? Or, if your daughter is spending time at a friend's house, is the friend's mother present? Even a birthday party for a five-year-old needs to be checked out in advance. Be on the alert for and avoid situations where parents are not present or won't closely supervise the get-together.

Train your daughter in social graces.

Training your girl in the social graces requires your time and attention. One of your goals as your daughter's social secretary is to teach her how to live successfully and productively. Be sure to train her, then, in the art of hospitality. Involve her in preparing food, setting the table, greeting and serving guests. Teach her how to be introduced and how to introduce herself. She'll feel more comfortable with people in social settings when she knows what to do. Train your daughter to live her Christianity with strength and dignity. The Proverbs 31 woman's character is your goal for your little or big girl: "Strength and honor are her clothing...She opens her mouth with wisdom, and on her tongue is the law of kindness" (verses 25-26).

Teach your daughter to choose God's standards.

Your daughter will always be your little girl, whether she's five or fifty. Today you are responsible for her social life, and hopefully you have it under control. But one day she will want to start making choices for herself. This is natural and normal. Commit to doing your job and instilling God's standards in her heart and mind. Pray that when she has the opportunity to make some or all of her own social decisions, she will choose the right kinds of friends, activities, and husband should she happen to marry.

Mom's Think Pad

Before you move on to your next Mom Mission, take a minute or two to think about what you can do to track with God as a mom. Make some plans of your own to take a few small steps that can make a big difference.

1. "Lord, today my daughter is _____ years old. I want to pray regularly for her friends and her best friends. Here are their names. Help my daughter to be a blessing to them, and help them to be a blessing to my daughter."

2. My daughter is a precious treasure. I need to make sure I am a functioning, caring social secretary for her activities. The first thing I'm going to do to be a better watch-mom is…

3. I've read the scriptures in this chapter that describe what kinds of people are to be friends with my girl—and those who are not an option. I need to go over these Bible passages with my daughter. Here's when I'm planning to sit down with her and show her what I've learned:

4. Am I in a hurry for my daughter to grow up? To dress and act like she's older? Am I rushing things? "Search my heart, Lord. Help me to enjoy these early years of sweet mommy-and-me times." When can I schedule a time for the two of us to have some girl time?

5. I need to make a list of important lessons to teach my daughter about social situations here in the neighborhood, at school, and when she's with other girls. To start my list, here are three things I must talk to her or warn her about:

Chapter 7

The Teacher

Part 1—The Model

Be reverent in behavior, not slanderers,
not given to much wine, teachers of good things.

—Titus 2:3

Now—I haven't looked into the mirror of my past for a l-o-n-g time! Maybe that's because of my desire to forget those things which are behind, reach forward to the things of today, and press on toward the goal for the prize of the upward call of God in Christ Jesus (Philippians 3:13-14). But today, as I step into this chapter about what a mom after God's own heart is to model before the daughter she is raising to follow God, I'm thinking back on my own years of growing up as a girl.

Believe me, the parade of activities that march by in my memory is quite an assortment. It's all over the map. I took piano and violin lessons. Every summer I added swim and tennis classes to my schedule. I joined ballet and tap-dancing classes, and later took ballroom dancing lessons—and more!

As I look at this list of past activities, I am reliving my time in each endeavor. I am recalling the teachers and leaders, where I sat in each class or studio, my peers who were there with me. I have to say I'm grateful for this quick review of the past and the opportunities my schoolteacher parents provided for me at great financial sacrifice to them. I can see how each pursuit contributed some strengthening element in my social development as a girl becoming a woman. Today I love music and play the piano enough to help out in our church's third-grade Sunday school class. I know a little about a lot of things. And as one of my brothers pointed out not long ago, I have a measure of what he called "poise" in life situations. (I had never thought about that before, but it was nice to hear coming from someone who was simply being forthright.)

I know you'll want to give your dear daughter opportunities to try to taste a number of educational experiences. Hopefully some of her tries will stick and she may even become proficient. For instance, one of my granddaughters started out as a beginner taking violin lessons and is now playing in the Hawaii Youth Symphony. Her stint of lessons stuck and struck home. So, by all means, round out your daughter's education if you can. But not at the expense of teaching and modeling for her what she needs to know about being a girl, a young woman, and a woman who follows God with all her heart.

Being the Real Thing

As you already know, you, mom, hold many vital titles—and roles—in your daughter's life. By God's design, *you* are the bell sheep, the prayer warrior, and the sower of seed, along with being both coach and trainer, the church lady, and the social secretary. And here now is yet another function you absolutely cannot neglect, that of being the model of good things for your daughter. This mission comes from Titus 2:3-5, where God records ten lifetime goals for all Christian women.

The premise of these three instructive verses is that the female population of the church, the body of Christ, is made up of older women and younger women. "Older" means older in age, and can also mean older and wiser in spiritual maturity. And "younger" refers to those who are younger in age and spiritual maturity.

When it comes to you and your daughter, *you* are her own private, built-in personal-gift-from-God resident older woman. And I must add, you are her Number One for-life teacher of good things. You live with her. You love her more than any other woman in all the world. You care deeply and desperately about her well-being and growth and progress in all areas. You are not only her mother, but her model!

If you're wondering what God considers crucial information for you to pass on to your girl, this chapter will help. Before we get specific, read Titus 2:3-5. This passage lists for you all ten essentials. And be sure to notice where the focus is *not*.

> The older women likewise, that they be reverent in behavior, not slanderers, not given to much wine, teachers of good things—that they admonish the young women to love their husbands, to love their children, to be discreet, chaste, homemakers, good, obedient to their own husbands, that the word of God may not be blasphemed.

As I just ran through this list of what *God* says is all-important in my life as a Christian woman, my first thought was, *All those lessons I took as a girl may have contributed to my "poise," but they had little or nothing to do with my character.* (How's that for a look at the past?)

Are you hearing God's challenge? For you to teach this spectacular lineup of character qualities to your daughter, you must first possess them yourself. You've probably heard the saying, "You cannot impart what you do not possess." So open your heart and pray to be the real thing. Ask God for the commitment, time, and passion to pass these after-God's-own-heart qualities on to your daughter.

Now let's look at verse 3. This is where you'll find the first four traits that you and I as moms are to live out and model day by day.

Mom as a Model

Lesson #1—Model Excellent Behavior

A woman and mom after God's own heart is to be "reverent in behavior." *Dignity* is a good word for "reverent." Other good words are *honorable* and *worthy of honor*. The best description is *Christlike*. And many people automatically refer to this quality as *godliness*. In short, everything about a woman of dignity is appropriate or suitable for a woman who is sold out to Jesus and wholeheartedly lives for Him.

So God gives moms an assignment: We are to seek this quality of dignified, godly behavior for ourselves and live it. When we do, we naturally and beautifully model godliness for our daughters. Your example is a guide your daughter can follow and live out in the same way. This character quality involves treating all people with respect and courtesy. So, mom, when you treat people with dignity, you are modeling how Jesus loved and treated people. You show your daughter that respect, good manners, and etiquette are still in style.

What can you do? Take the spiritual temperature of your own heart. When Jesus, with "eyes like a flame of fire" (Revelation 1:14) assessed the spiritual condition of the people in the church in Ephesus, He charged, "I know your works, that you are neither cold nor hot. I could wish you were cold or hot. So then, because you are lukewarm, and neither cold nor hot, I will vomit you out of My mouth" (Revelation 3:15-16).

We teach more by what we do and don't do than by what we say.

Jesus labeled these people's hearts as "lukewarm." This means they were probably hot-hearted at one time, but somewhere along the way, their hearts began to cool down toward the things of God. Here's a thought and a saying: "The coals are hottest which are closest to the fire." If you want your daughter to have a "hot heart" for Jesus, then you must draw near to Jesus' flame with all your heart. If you want your daughter to be godly and Christlike, then show her the way. Be hot-hearted yourself. Be on fire for Jesus.

Lesson #2—Model Uplifting Speech

Oh boy—here we go! Titus 2:3 says older women are supposed to be "not slanderers," or "not malicious gossips" (NASB). Unfortunately this seems to be a weakness for females, for this matter is addressed repeatedly in the Bible. It's true that we l-o-v-e to talk! And the more we talk, the higher the odds are that we'll gossip. That's what the Bible says in Proverbs 10:19: "In the multitude of words sin is not lacking, but he who restrains his lips is wise." Or, "when words are many, sin is not absent, but he who holds his tongue is wise" (NIV).

Once again, as you well know, we teach more by what we do and don't do than by what we say. So, mom, when you don't participate in gossip and slander, your silence speaks more loudly than a thousand lectures to you daughter on how she should not be a gossip girl.

So the first step to modeling excellence in speech is mom's mouth. If your daughter never hears you gossip or put down others, she will be positively influenced by your sweet speech. And when she is treated to witnessing your compassion and hearing your admiration of others, she'll be positively influenced by your Christlikeness. Remember, Jesus loved any and all. He loved His family, His 12 disciples, and the poor, the oppressed, the afflicted. And He loved sinners. Instead of verbally tearing people to shreds, He healed them, provided for them, comforted them, and opened the door to eternal life. Instead of being destructive through gossip and slander, Jesus "went about doing good" (Acts 10:38).

It's scary to realize that your daughter hears what you say about others when you talk on the phone or to her dad, when you chat with another woman or talk to her about another person. I personally had to learn *not* to gossip. I have written about my struggle at length in several of my books. My mouth was poison—skull-and-crossbones poison. My words killed. That's what slander and gossip means—to pull down, tear down, cut down another person's reputation. To kill their good name in the eyes of others. To ruin a person's honor and good estimation held by others.

Once you decide it's okay for you to put people down, talk about them, share their faults and failures, and pass judgment on them, guess what? Your sweet innocent daughter will begin to do the same. But God says you are to do the opposite—to be her teacher of *good* things.

What can you do? Name gossip for what it is—sin. The Bible says, "Don't gossip." So when you do, confess it as sin right away (1 John 1:9). Then, together with your daughter, set some of these anti-gossip tactics in motion:

Think the best about others—Gossip is an issue of the heart. That means when you gossip, the ugliness in your heart is revealed. Instead apply the principles of Philippians 4:8 and think things about people that are true, noble, just, pure, lovely, of good report, excellent, and worthy of praise.

Stay away from others who gossip—Maybe you know women and girls who gossip all the time and easily draw others into their web of meanness. They delight in gathering and passing on information that hurts others. Be strong and learn to excuse yourself and walk away.

Avoid settings where gossip usually occurs—For you, mom, activities like meetings, a lunch out, riding in the car or shopping with another woman, or even the simple act of picking up your daughter from school and visiting with the other moms can be a breeding ground for gossip. And for your daughter, gatherings around the lockers in the hall at school or during lunch hour, as well as long talks or text messages on the phone and parties and sleepovers provide hundreds of opportunities for gossip. Tell your daughter to be aware, be on guard, and pray before she finds herself in a difficult situation.

Say nothing—You may have heard the military slogan "Loose lips sink ships." Those who serve in the armed forces are constantly cautioned to say nothing in public about their job. The reason? The more they talk, the more likely they will say something they shouldn't. The same is true for you and your daughter. The surest way to keep from gossiping is to say nothing.

Lesson #3—Model Self-discipline

The wording of this quality in Titus 2:3, "not given to much wine," may sound a little strange. But it refers to a time and culture when wine was safer to drink than water. So of course it was easy for anyone to drink more than was necessary. Therefore God issued the warning that women were to be careful not to drink too much wine. They were cautioned not to become addicted to wine. In other words, they were to exercise self-control.

This principle of personal discipline broadens out to include any beverage, as well as food or anything else, that a person could become addicted to or overindulge in. In my own life, I've had my bouts with coffee addiction. And other women I know need their cola, or their chocolate, or their favorite brand of chips. You name it—when it comes to the things we like, it's frighteningly easy to form bad habits.

And there's more! Here's a composite of what temperance and self-control mean:

> not addicted to alcoholic beverages (or anything else),
>
> controlled in our actions and words,
>
> mild and calm in our emotions,
>
> lacking in extremes and extravagance, and
>
> serious in our behavior.[18]

What can you do? *First, remember self-control is a fruit of the Spirit* (Galatians 5:23). When you are controlled by God's Spirit, you will exhibit personal discipline. You will have the inner power of the Holy Spirit to help you choose what to think and not think, what to say and not say, what to do and not do. Looking to God's Spirit will guide you to do all things, "whether you eat or drink, or whatever you do...to the glory of God" (1 Corinthians 10:31).

Second, restrict yourself in your weak areas. What is your biggest problem when it comes to personal discipline and self-control? Or what area do you need to take on next? Name it and get to work on it so you can model it for your daughter. With God's power as your resource, victory is

A daughter who has the privilege of witnessing a mom making Spirit-filled choices, honoring and glorifying God with the choices she makes, is doubly blessed.

always available. And remember, there is always room for growth. You'll be tackling one area of discipline after another until the day you meet the Lord face-to-face.

A daughter who has a mom who even cares about personal discipline is extremely fortunate. And a daughter who has the privilege of witnessing a mom making Spirit-filled choices, honoring and glorifying God with the choices she makes, is doubly blessed.

Lesson #4—Model What Is Good

Whether we like it or not, we moms teach by everything we say and do, and everything we don't say and do. Teaching is not the hard thing. The hard thing is *what* we are teaching. Is it good or bad? Is it helpful or harmful?

God answers these questions right here in Titus 2:3. He instructs us moms to make double-sure that what we teach our young daughters is "good"—virtuous, right, and noble—and nothing but. We are to be sharing God's wisdom, knowledge, and faith. What we pass on to our daughters is to be useful, helpful, and excellent. It's godly instruction that He wants us to pass down from our generation to the next...and the next. This means your home is the natural classroom for this kind of instruction to take place.

Spiritual training takes top priority. Never lose sight of your goal—it is to raise a daughter after God's own heart. As much as it is up to you, have family devotions. And help your daughter have her own personal time for devotions. Make it a goal to shop for and purchase whatever Christian resources are age-appropriate and helpful to your girl.

If your daughter is still a baby, hold her in your lap and say, "Let's spend time with Jesus!" And for toddlers, get a picture Bible and activity books and keep on spending time with Jesus. Be right there with her. Lead her through her little colorful Bible and give her a little activity or sticker book about the Bible. Make this time together fun, fun, fun!

When your daughter learns to read, be sure she has a Bible and books about Jesus that are on her reading level. Encourage her to ask you questions and to share and articulate the truths she's learning. Again, what's important is that you be a part of her spiritual journey.

And as she matures, teach her to have her own alone-time with God. Then make it a point to periodically sit together over a smoothie or a mug of hot chocolate or a glass of lemonade and let her talk about what she is learning. Another growth-encourager is getting her a cool journal or diary in which she can write about the discoveries she makes as she does her daily Bible reading.

Oh, and don't forget to teach her how to pray! This is yet another "good thing" you can do to fulfill God's calling for you in Titus 2:3. If your daughter is still a baby, teach her to put her head on folded hands when you say grace at each meal. As she grows older, let her pray her own personal prayers. And as she grows up, help her prayers grow up in content too. Let her hear you pray. And show her how to create her very own prayer notebook or journal. Girls love to write...and write...and write!

And then there's church. Don't forget to involve her in service and ministry opportunities there. I'm assuming you as "the church lady" are, of course, getting your girl to church. But more than that, as she grows up, let her come alongside and help you as you serve at your church—whether you help set things up or take them down, bake snacks, or teach a class. Allow your daughter to be your personal assistant. And when she's the right age, let her help care for and teach little ones in the nursery or toddler class. Encourage her to become "a teacher of good things."

Just for You, Mom

This is a great place to pause and think—and pray!—about what Titus 2:3 is all about. Of the ten essentials for a woman, mom, and daughter after God's own heart that are named in Titus 2:3-5, these first four are just for you, mom. They are the four qualities that must be in your life before you can teach them to your daughter, before you can truly show her how to follow God with all her heart.

This makes every day a challenge, doesn't it? As if being a mom isn't enough of a challenge already! But you can do it! You *can* work on Christlike behavior as you grow in knowledge and the application of God's Word. You *can* put perimeters around your speech and stop talking about people in negative ways. You *can* ask God for help with self-control. And you *can*—and will *love*—spending time with your daughter and sharing the good things out of God's Word together as a mother and daughter. In fact, you will find yourself wanting your own journal so you can make a record of all of the thrilling times the two of you enjoy together!

The Teacher

Part 2—The Mentor

Admonish the young women to love their husbands,
to love their children, to be discreet,
chaste, homemakers, good...
that the word of God may not be blasphemed.

—TITUS 2:4-5

The mentor. Have you ever wondered about the history behind this practice? It's fascinating. Let's take a minute to look at it as we continue to address the subject of mentoring your daughter—of teaching her the qualities she needs to live a life that honors the Lord.

In the eighth century BC, the poet Homer wrote in his major Greek work, *The Odyssey*, about a man named *Mentor*. Mentor was the friend of the warrior Odysseus. When Odysseus went off to fight in the Trojan War, Mentor was left in charge of Odysseus's household. This meant he was obligated to teach, tutor, and protect Telemachus, Odysseus's son. Mentor was responsible to his mandate to train Telemachus until his father returned many years later.

As we return to discovering what Titus 2:3-5 tells us to teach our daughters, think about Mentor. He faithfully mentored a boy who was not his son. But you, dear mom, get to mentor your very own daughter! In the same way that Odysseus put Mentor in charge of training his son, so God has put you in charge of training your daughter.

In the previous chapter, we looked at what you are to impart to your daughter as a role model. Now let's consider your calling as her mentor.

Mom as a Mentor

Lesson #5—Love Your Husband

Maybe your little girl is just learning to walk, and here we are talking about marriage—eek! Don't freak out. Listen to this: I cut out and saved an article from a newspaper about teaching music. It said, "The time to start a child on a musical career isn't too far beyond the bootie and bottle age." If music experts are telling us to start teaching our children music at an early age, then why shouldn't you, mom, start early? Only you're not going to focus on music. You get to begin teaching biblical principles, especially that of love! God is love, and He wants His women to manifest that quality too.

So who are we to love besides the Lord?

Titus 2:4 begins by telling us that a married woman is to love her husband. Wrapped up in that love is a willingness to help him with his responsibilities, follow his leadership, and respect him as a person.[19] As you demonstrate love and respect to your husband, your daughter will see firsthand what kind of wife she should be (if marriage is God's will for her).

The key to teaching and mentoring your daughter about how to love a future husband (again, if that is God's will for her) is to tend to your own heart and marriage. Each day that you wake up is a day to assist, support, honor, and adore your hubby, your daughter's dad. It's vital that you show this kind of love because God asks you to and expects you to. It's what a wife after God's own heart does! And don't forget, your little girl is watching. She won't miss a thing! Your loving actions are training her for the future. She's seeing it. She's hearing it. She's filing it away and taking it to heart.

Modeling a wife's love for her husband is important, but you also need to show your daughter what a godly man looks like. So, like the music teacher said, start now. Don't wait until emotions cloud your daughter's judgment. Begin painting a picture for her of qualities she should look for in the boys she pals with. A great place to find God's guidelines for future and potential romantic relationships is the book of Ruth. Take time to talk about the qualities highlighted in Boaz, the man Ruth came to marry. Your daughter should hold out for a man who is...

> *Godly*—He has a passion for Jesus. This should be #1 on her list. Boaz prayed for Ruth and asked God to bless her (2:12).
>
> *Diligent*—He is a hard worker. Boaz was a careful manager of his property and wealth (2:1).
>
> *Friendly*—He is the kind of guy who will always be a friend. Boaz gave a warm greeting and welcome to Ruth as she entered his field (2:4,8).
>
> *Merciful*—He has great compassion for others. Boaz asked about Ruth's situation as a widow and acted on her behalf and in her best interest (2:7).
>
> *Encouraging*—He positively encourages her growth in spiritual matters, character development, educational and personal interests (2:12; 3:11).
>
> *Generous*—He has a giving heart. Ruth needed food and worked hard for it. Boaz saw that, appreciated it, and arranged for her to be given extra food (2:15).
>
> *Kind*—He's possesses a kind heart. Boaz obviously cared for Ruth's well-being. He also cared for Ruth's mother-in-law, Naomi. Naomi thanked God for Boaz's kindness toward her and Ruth (2:20).
>
> *Discreet*—He protects her reputation. Ruth went to see Boaz in the evening, and he honored her purity (3:14).
>
> *Faithful*—He keeps his word. Boaz followed through on his promise to marry Ruth (4:1,10).[20]

Boaz sounds like a great guy, doesn't he? He models the kind of man you and your daughter should be praying for as her future husband. As time passes, help your daughter to be patient. Help her wait for Mr. Right. He's out there! Until he comes along, make sure she's preparing herself to be Miss Right. A godly guy will have high standards. Your job is to mentor your daughter to have high standards too—the ones God set for her.

Lesson #6—Love Your Children

Titus 2:4 goes on to say that moms are to "love their children." Every chapter in this book shines the spotlight on a variety of wonderful ways you are to love your daughter. And each one of these ways is something you, as a mom who loves her, are to teach and model.

Maybe you're sitting there holding this book and thinking, *I can't take on one more thing—I'm on overload as it is!* Well, let me encourage you. Sure, every mommy has her bad days, days of challenge. Raising children is not easy. Every mom will say "Amen!" to that. You've got diapers, food preparation, sickness...and laundry galore! It's never fun or a pleasure to discipline. And teaching and training and caring for your kids fills every day to the brim. It's 24/7—day and night, and night and day...*every* day! Even when they're not with you physically, your children occupy your thoughts and emotions. You are to love your children, no matter what.

But all that you do in the midst of the busyness, chaos, and heartbreak *is* your love in action. *Love* is not giving up. *Love* is not quitting. *Love* is not turning your heart off. *Love* is not screaming your head off. No, love prevails. And that is what Titus 2:4 is telling you and me. We are to love our children no matter what.

If there's no sacrifice, there's no gain. And the gain you are looking for is the joy of fulfilling God's mandate to you to raise a daughter after God's own heart. Your time and energy can be spent on nothing more important or satisfying than this mission from God. Giving your all to this God-given assignment is a truly worthwhile pursuit. This, my friend, is love.

So hang in there. Pray for the wisdom and strength to do what God asks of you, and then do it. Mentor your daughter! Teach her godly character qualities—the ones listed in Titus 2:3-5. This is love. How can I say that? Because godly character will shield her during those turbulent teen years. It will sustain her as she leaves the shelter of your home and ventures out into the world to start her own family, or enter the workforce, or serve as a missionary in a far-off land.

Lesson #7—Be Discreet

Discreet. Are you unsure exactly what that means? How about sensible, sober-minded, reasonable, wise, and orderly? What a trait! If you were looking at a woman who is acting discreetly, you would be witnessing a woman who doesn't lose it—doesn't lose her temper, her cool, her mind, her mouth, or her control. She's a walking picture of wisdom in her choices and actions. She's careful. She's got her priorities in order, and she lives them out. She knows what's important and devotes herself to those few concerns instead of the many lesser, trivial matters that so often weigh us down.

I like to think of a woman of discretion as having her head screwed on right. She knows who she is and what it is she does and is supposed to do.

And who is she? A Christian. This constant reminder dictates her values, commitments, and conduct.

And what is it she does and is supposed to do? One of her primary goals is raising a daughter after God's own heart.

So what does it take to get your head screwed on right? Here's what I've learned: It requires getting into God's Word. This one choice will tune your heart to God's. It will remind you of His vision and perspective on your limited time and energy. It will cause you to look at your day through His eyes. That, in turn, will lead you to plan your day and make decisions that work out His grand plan for you instead of frittering it away on insignificant activities. You will view your life as He does. And you'll respond to whatever comes your way as He would respond—with His "love, joy, peace, longsuffering, kindness, goodness, faithfulness, gentleness, self-control" (Galatians 5:22-23).

Now, once you've got the definition of discretion down and are attempting to live it out, you are to mentor your daughter in that same character quality. You are to teach her to be discreet, or wise.

And how do you help your daughter toward this goal of being wise? Here's what I've learned from mentoring my two girls...who are now mentoring their four girls.

First, get your daughter into God's Word. The Bible will reinforce what you are telling her—and she will realize these principles are coming from God Himself. Let her experience the joy of spiritual growth. Let her "senses [be] exercised to discern both good and evil" (Hebrews 5:14). Then teach her how to plan her day. Help her learn how to set daily goals and guard her time so she can achieve those goals.

And by all means, show your daughter the ropes when it comes to making decisions. Here's a short checklist for decision-making. Each time she has a decision to make, encourage her to ask these questions and look at these verses:

1. Will it be legal (1 Peter 2:13-15)?

2. Will my parents approve (Ephesians 6:1)?

3. Will it cause others to stumble (1 Corinthians 8:12-13)?

4. Will it benefit others (1 Corinthians 6:12)?

5. Will it become habit-forming (1 Corinthians 6:12)?

6. Will it help me to grow (1 Corinthians 10:23)?

7. Will it be a good testimony (1 Peter 2:12)?

8. Will it glorify God (1 Corinthians 10:31)?

Lesson #8—Be Chaste

Oh boy! Does that sound old-fashioned? Well, let's consider other terms that paint a picture of what God has in mind when He urges us to "be...chaste" (Titus 2:5). How about free from sin? Innocent? Pure?

Whenever anyone mentions purity, what usually comes to your mind? Sexual purity, right? And it's true you should discuss this key area of life with your daughter. Her physical purity is important to God. He makes it very clear in His Word that He wants all Christian women—young and old, single and married—to be pure in body.

But purity extends beyond just saying no to sex outside of

marriage. It also has to do with what you and your daughter put into your bodies. It includes making the right choices about smoking, drinking alcohol, and taking drugs. And it includes what you see and hear. You, as a mentor, must teach your daughter to do what you do to scrutinize and watch over her sexual purity. That's square one. Tell her how to guard her thoughts, her practices, and her vocabulary so she remains pure in heart. Let her know how vital it is that she be hypercautious about what she reads, sees, and hears—what she exposes herself to, and who her close friends are.

You and your daughter are up against peer pressure—serious peer pressure! But God-pressure and pleasing Him is greater.

As a mom and mentor, do for your daughter what you do for yourself. Watch over, point out, and discuss with her what you consider to be inappropriate language, conduct, and clothing—anything that doesn't match up to God's standard of purity and chasteness.

And here's something that's not news to you. You and your daughter are up against peer pressure—serious peer pressure! But God-pressure and pleasing Him is greater. The day may come (or is already here) when you will find yourself going head to head with your daughter as she is being lured into succumbing to the norm at school or among other girls. But, as in all other things, remember that *you* are the mom. God has chosen *you* to teach your very own daughter His good things—things that will protect her and grow her into a woman after God's own heart.

So what can you do? Love your daughter, pray faithfully for her, listen to her, talk with her, enjoy her, and have fun with her. And when it comes to purity, help her to know and understand that this is God's will for her. Be persistent. You are in charge of what she watches on television at home. You are in charge of her wardrobe, of what she has in her closet and drawers. You are in charge of those she spends time with apart from school. And you are in charge of what's accessed online on the family computer. So do your part, mom. *Really* do it! Be a mentor. And pray like crazy. You have God on your side. So plead with Him to work in your daughter's heart.

Lesson #9—Be Homemakers

Home, sweet home! Everybody wants one and everybody needs one. And now God is telling His moms and daughters and all women to make it happen. Titus 2:5 says we are to be "homemakers," or as other meanings of this term say, "keepers at home," "homekeepers," "house-keepers," "to keep house," and "home lovers."

I personally prefer the last one—"home lovers." I tell my Jim every day, "Do you know what makes a great day for me? Doing something special to our home." I *love* being a keeper of our home! This was not always true. One day, after eight years of marriage, I woke up and realized we were living in a pigsty. As a new Christian, I came across this quality as I read Titus chapter 2 in my new Bible. Well, that day I ran out and purchased several books on homemaking and organization. I also started meeting with other women from the church to find out how they maintained their homes. And I've been richly blessed since—not only because these women were willing to help me—mentor me—but also because I now experience daily the joy that comes from taking care of my home.

And I mentored my two girls to do the same. Believe me, they've far surpassed me as homemakers, and I'm thrilled.

And guess what? I started them early. You can start as early as showing your toddler how to put her toys away, or put her blanket in a special place during the day. I've seen my little toddling granddaughters put their shoes in a neat row. Girls can also make their beds "all pretty." Every child can carry dishes to the kitchen counter to help out Mom. Your little one can stand on a stepstool and put her clothes in the washer. As time goes by, she can learn how to load and unload the dishwasher (or even wash and dry dishes by hand). You can show her how to vacuum, dust, and empty wastebaskets. And this is just the beginning of teaching housecleaning skills, food preparation, hospitality and entertaining, and on and on.

So, whether your daughter is two or twenty-two, you are to communicate to her that keeping her own space neat and clean is not just a rule for living in your home. It's God's rule. Here are two simple how-to's for mentoring her in the home-sweet-home department.

TEACH YOUR DAUGHTER THE BASICS OF HOUSEWORK

There are only a handful of basics involved in taking care of your daughter's room or her part of the room if she shares with a sister. They are dusting, vacuuming, cleaning, doing laundry, and organizing. And like any skill, these are learned by repetition. The more she does them, the easier they become—until they are habits that she will carry out all through her life.

I taught my daughters these basics, and together the three of us did them over and over and over until we were able to do them quickly. Then miracle of miracles, when the girls got married, guess what? Homemaking was no big deal. Because they had already mastered the basics as a result of taking care of their own little areas of the house, they had already formed their homemaking skills by the time they moved into their own homes.

TEACH YOUR DAUGHTER THE BASICS OF FOOD PREPARATION

I had a very unusual home-life growing up. My mother was an English teacher who always had lots of papers to grade. My dad was a vocational teacher whose work was done when he left the school. So my dad cooked our meals, did the laundry, and took care of most of the housework.

Enter my Jim...followed by a wedding...followed by a move into our first apartment. At last the day arrived when I was supposed to cook a meal. I decided I would "cook" beans and cornbread. What could be so hard about that, right? I wish you could have seen the look on Jim's face when he took his first bite of beans! All I can say is, how was I supposed to know I needed to wash the sand and grit out of the beans before I cooked them?

Needless to say, Jim lost a few pounds before I got things turned around. But here's the point: A homemaker prepares food for her family. She cooks. So, as you have probably guessed, I made sure my two daughters not only knew how to take care of their homes, but also how to cook!

Lesson #10—Be Good

Goodness—which is yet another quality listed in Titus 2:3-5 for being a woman after God's own heart and for raising a daughter after God's own heart—is high on God's list of character qualities.

It is mentioned twice in these three verses: Older women are to be teachers of "good things" (verse 3) so they can teach the young women to be "good" (verse 5). This word could also be translated as "kind." So our mission as moms includes teaching our daughters to be good, kind, gentle, considerate, and sympathetic toward others. If you are looking for an example from the Bible, look at the Proverbs 31 woman: "She does [her husband] *good* and not evil all the days of her life," and "she opens her mouth with wisdom, and on her tongue is the law of *kindness*" (Proverbs 31:12,26).

As you go about the business of training your daughter to be amiable and congenial, take a look in your mirror. Is the law of kindness on your heart? Are you easy to be around, or do people (including your family members) have to walk on eggshells when they are around you? Are you Mrs. Grumpy or Mrs. Congeniality? Goodness and kindness, mom, all begin with you. Read through the following steps for cultivating kindness and goodness, and make sure they are part of your daily routine. Then, of course, you'll want to help your daughter add them to her routine.

> *Prepare your heart for kindness*—Nothing so prepares the way for a day of goodness and kindness as time spent in God's Word.
>
> *Pray for kindness*—As you ask, seek, and knock on God's door in prayer, be sure to include asking for a heart that seeks to do good. Ask Him to give you greater love and compassion for others, beginning right at home.
>
> *Plan for kindness*—Take out your daily planner and write, "How can I show kindness to each one in my family today?" The very act of writing this down will prompt you to look for opportunities to reach out to those under your own roof all day long.
>
> *Put away what is not kind*—Unfortunately our hearts are "desperately wicked" (Jeremiah 17:9). It's soooo easy to slip back into our old habits. So God tells us not to give in to the old life, but to "put off... anger, wrath, malice, blasphemy, filthy language"

(Colossians 3:8). In other words, "rid yourselves of all such things" (NIV).

Put on a heart of kindness—Now, dear mom, put on your new Christlike wardrobe! "Put on tender mercies, [and] kindness" (verse 12). Live out this quality, and pass it on to your daughter.

Highlights for the Heart

I hope you are not feeling overwhelmed. Be encouraged! God gives you a lifetime to learn and live out the content of Titus 2:3-5. These verses span the entirety of a woman's life and ministry. I'm praying you will embrace your mission as one of God's moms. Your goal? Model the right kind of behavior, speech, and personal discipline, and mentor your daughter in what is good—purity, wisdom, goodness, and love for her home and the people in her life. These few but significant qualities are to make up the core of your character as mom and daughter.

As I was writing this, I received an incredible e-mail from a mom of an eight-year-old, a six-year-old, and a five-month-old. At last, after eight years of being a mom, she realized that the world was affecting her children and her home, and she decided to roll up her mothering sleeves and take action! I can't say it enough: It's never too early—or too late (this mom is just getting started)—to begin modeling and teaching the ten character qualities God desires for you as the mom of a young woman after God's own heart in the making.

You Can Do It!

Each of the following suggestions is something you can do to contribute toward becoming the mom you dream of being. And each one betters your life...and your daughter's too. Here we go:

Make mentoring your daughter a priority.

When something is important to you, you'll have no problem finding the time to do it. So how important is helping your daughter become a woman after God's heart? You probably make a schedule every day. So start planning a time when you'll get together with your daughter on a daily basis. You are in charge of your time, so make time with your girl happen. It's a priority. And isn't God gracious? He isn't asking you to teach your daughter 100 things or even 50 things. He has given—in Titus 2:3-5—only ten qualities that will point her toward becoming a woman after His own heart. Surely you have time for that!

Teach your daughter godly qualities.

We teach our daughters a lot of things. How to gift wrap a box. How to do a craft. How to braid their hair. How to drive! But as a mentor for God, make teaching your daughter the ten essentials of Titus 2:3-5 a top priority. Put it on the top of your "Things I Need to Teach My Daughter" list. She is your stewardship. Be sure you don't leave a huge gap in her education. Fill her heart with the "good things" you've been learning from Titus 2:3-5.

Enlist the resources of others.

God doesn't expect you to know everything or provide all the mentoring your daughter will ever receive. But He does expect you to do the majority of the teaching, both by your words and your life example. Read your Bible. Read parenting books. And read books about cultivating godly character—books you can share with your daughter. Find Christian books for little girls, young girls, and teens that will speak to your daughter's heart. Talk to mothers who have already raised their daughters and moms who are in the throes of raising their girls. You are not alone!

Live consistently.

Your home is a transparent classroom. That's good and bad, because your daughter is watching. She'll notice when what you preach doesn't match up with what you practice. So be on guard, on alert, on your toes, and most of all, on your knees. Live out what a loving wife and mom looks like, and one day your daughter may add these two roles to her life. Watch over your mouth and your habits: You are contributing to hers. Take care of your home: You have a homemaker-in-the-making living right under your roof. And be a model of all that is good, wise, and pure: These qualities will take her through life.

Read from Proverbs.

Solomon wrote the book of Proverbs to teach his child—his young son—wisdom. The proverbs were meant to instruct his son in the disciplines he would need throughout life. Doesn't that sound like something your daughter might need? So give her the gift of the proverbs. Give her godly wisdom. How? Read one chapter of Proverbs every day yourself, the chapter that matches the day of the month. When the month is over, start all over again. And teach your daughter to do this too. You can even try to read Proverbs out loud together as often as possible. This golden wisdom will become a part of your lives, and will guide you both "in the way [you] should go" (Proverbs 22:6).

Mom's Think Pad

Before you move on to your next Mom Mission, take a minute or two to think about what you can do to track with God as a mom. Make some plans of your own to take a few small steps that can make a big difference.

1. So I'm to be both a model and a mentor to my girl. As I scan back through parts 1 and 2 of chapter 7, and as I look through this list of ten "good things," I'm a little overwhelmed when I realize that God has called me to teach my daughter...

     —excellent and godly behavior

     —uplifting and godly speech

     —self-discipline

     —good and godly things

     —the role of a wife

     —the role of a mother

     —wisdom and discretion

     —purity in all areas of life

     —how to make and care for a home

     —goodness and kindness

   First, myself. Teaching my daughter starts with me. As I consider this list, here are three areas where I need to do a better job myself:

     —

     —

     —

And now for my daughter. As of today, she is _____ years old. Considering her age, I need to zero in on teaching her more about these three qualities:

—

—

—

2. Even though I feel like my time and energies are already maxed out, mentoring my daughter deserves my time. I need to take some action!

—This week I need to make a list of books to read in the future that will help me raise my daughter to follow God. I'll put it on my to-do list now.

—This week I need to make a schedule that includes specific time slots for teaching my girl. I'll put it on my to-do list now.

—"Right now, Father God, I lift this prayer to You. It is an expression of my desire to take my responsibility of model and mentor to my daughter more seriously. I write it with my own hand and heart (place your prayer here):

Chapter 8

The Homebuilder

The wise woman builds her house.

—Proverbs 14:1

When I think about my growing-up days, it seems like my parents had two sets of children. They had two sons, then after a gap of six and seven years, they had one more son and me! By the time I married Jim, my dad was already retirement age. That meant it wouldn't be too many years before we would need to set up assisted living arrangements for my parents.

Well, that's exactly what happened. It was then that some amazing things took place. When the time came, my brothers and I—without any of us knowing what the others were doing—all invited our parents to live with us. And my parents sweetly declined each one of us. They had lived for what seemed like forever in their hometown in a house they had practically built with their own hands, and they could not bear the thought of leaving (let alone dealing with a lifetime of accumulated household items!).

Ultimately my dad and mom chose to move into assisted living facilities. Then when my dad became terminally ill with cancer and was dying, none of his children wanted him to be alone even for a single day. So together we four siblings worked out a solution and a plan. My brothers with careers could trade off weekends with my father. But the weekdays were a problem. So Jim and I agreed that I could and should fly from Los Angeles to Oklahoma each week, Monday through Thursday, to sit at my dad's bedside. Our nest was empty, and Jim strongly felt this was a real way to live out God's desire that we "honor" my father.

Little did any of us ever imagine this tag-team effort on our part would last for almost a year before my father passed away.

I'm relating this story only because it provides a perfect illustration of what's involved in treasuring the value of family. It also is an important principle that you, as a homebuilder who is raising a daughter after God's own heart, will want to model.

The First Law with a Promise

I know the answer to this question before I even ask it, but I'm going to ask anyway: If you could give your daughter advice that would assure her of a long and happy life, would you do whatever was necessary to get that promise across to her? Of course you would, and so would I! What loving mom wouldn't want this for her daughter?

And speaking of promises, it's been estimated that there are as many as 30,000 promises in the Bible. It's true that many of these promises are specific promises to specific people or groups of people, such as the nation of Israel. But there is one special promise from God that is for all people for all times—a promise given as part of the Ten Commandments: "Honor your father and your mother, that your days may be long upon the land" (Exodus 20:12). The apostle Paul referred to this as "the first commandment with [a] promise" (Ephesians 6:2).

Now, let's go to work on getting this all-important promise from God across to your daughter. And remember, God cannot lie (Titus 1:2). He will keep His word. But where does it all start? It starts with you as the homebuilder, with you as the "wise woman [who] builds her house"—on purpose, with diligence, and with a willing heart (Proverbs 14:1).

The Promise Lived Out

Moses is the man who wrote down the command to "honor

your father and your mother" as well as its glowing promise—"that your days may be long upon the land." There's no doubt Moses was one of the greatest men mentioned in the Bible. He was asked by God to lead a nation of over two million people out of Egypt and into the Promised Land. And he was given the Ten Commandments.

I could go on and on with interesting facts about Moses' position, power, and leadership. But I don't want to pass over what an ideal model he was of how we should love and honor family. He shows us the kind of love and relationships we should have with our parents, and drives home the importance of passing this on to the next generation.

Show Respect to Your Family

Moses' extended family included Jethro, his father-in-law. Moses married Jethro's daughter and became a sheepherder, caring for Jethro's flock. After 40 years of tending sheep, God asked Moses to make a career change. Notice the humility and respect Moses exhibited as he presented his request to leave his father-in-law: "Please, let me go and return to my brethren who are in Egypt, and see whether they are still alive."[21]

Through Moses' example, we learn that we're to be courteous toward our father and mother and other family members. Even after a divine call from God Himself, Moses, who was nearly 80 years old, still approached Jethro with a humble heart and a respectful attitude.

How can you teach your daughter this kind of respect? As "the homebuilder," demonstrate such honor yourself as you build positive, loving relationships at home. Show it daily toward your husband and your own parents and in-laws. Pride is a terrible attitude. It says, "I don't need you in my life." And neglect says, "I don't love you enough to think about you." These are definitely not the attitudes you want your daughter to develop toward you, her dad, and her brothers and sisters. She may not know it yet (and it's your job to teach her this), but family—even her goofy, bothersome little brother or sister—will always be a part of her life. Long after the friends she absolutely can't live a day without are gone, she will still have her family.

Honor Your Family

The next time we encounter Moses and his father-in-law is after the exodus of God's people from Egypt. With Jethro's blessing, Moses had gone to do as God requested, leaving his wife and two sons in Jethro's care. The day came when Jethro brought Moses' wife and two sons to meet up with him. Notice how the great leader of a nation of two million people greeted his father-in-law: "Moses went out to meet his father-in-law, bowed down, and kissed him" (Exodus 18:7). Admittedly, some of Moses' actions depict the culture of his day, but his example is quickly validated by God's commandment to "honor your father and your mother" (Exodus 20:12).

The courtesy and honor you exhibit toward your parents will speak volumes to your daughter.

How are you, mom, showing honor to your own parents and in-laws? When you are around them, does your daughter see you honor them verbally and with your attention and admiration? Yes, it's true you no longer live under your parents' roof. You have your own roof, your own home, and your own family unit to build. And no, you are not accountable to them. But God's command is for you to continue showing your love and esteem. The courtesy and honor you exhibit toward your parents will speak volumes to your daughter.

Stay Connected with Your Family

After Moses honored Jethro, he inquired about his father-in-law's welfare: "They asked each other about their well-being, and they went into the tent" to visit (Exodus 18:7). In other words, Moses was interested in his father-in-law's well-being and communicated it.

It's sad to say, but too many families today have relationship issues. Maybe a relative has hurt you or one of your family members and there's now a rift. I recently heard about a mother and daughter who hadn't spoken to each other in over 30 years. I don't know what happened, but I couldn't help but think, *This is so unnatural! And so sad. What a loss for that mom and her daughter. Just think of the grandchildren, who have never even met their grandmother, and the fact the grandmother has never seen her grandchildren.*

Dear mom, don't let a rift develop in your family. *You* are the homebuilder. You can't change another family member's heart, but you can certainly change yours. Ask God to warm your heart toward any estranged family member so you can rebuild the relationship. Do as the apostle Paul advises: "If it is possible, as far as it depends on you, live at peace with everyone" (Romans 12:18 NIV). And remember, "everyone" includes all your family and in-laws.

I know from firsthand experience that life gets very busy for moms and homebuilders. It's easy to get wrapped up in your responsibilities, interests, and even your own family. It's easy to sort of forget about your parents and brothers and sisters (unless they live across the street!). No, you didn't make a decision to stop communicating. It just happened.

Maybe it's time for a heart checkup. How often do you communicate with family? What is your interest level in your parents and in-laws? Do you call, write, or e-mail on a regular basis about their health, activities, and interests? Don't forget to reach out.

God says you are to *honor* your parents and parents-in-law. It's such an easy assignment! You honor them every time you think of them, pray for them, and communicate with them. And all of this honoring should involve your daughter. Let your daughter hear you talking positively about her grandparents, aunts, and uncles. Let her see you writing, calling, and visiting them. Take her along with you. When you do, not only is she treated to time with her grandparents, but some mother-daughter time as a bonus! By choosing to honor your parents, you teach your daughter that family is important. And someday, when your daughter is out on her own, hopefully you'll get the same treatment.

Be Friends with Your Family

Age differences between family members shouldn't keep you from being good friends with your parents, brothers, and sisters. There was an age gap between Moses and Jethro, yet the Bible shows them as being the greatest of friends. As Moses described the exodus to his father-in-law and the defeat of Pharaoh's army, Jethro praised God for the miraculous deliverance of Israel. These two men spent time with each other, time that focused upon rejoicing in God together (Exodus 18:8-12).

How close are you to your parents and siblings? Do you keep them up to date on what's happening with you and your family? Do you encourage your daughter to talk to them and tell them all that's going on in her life? As the homebuilder, decide that your children need to have a relationship with family, and make it happen. And be prepared—this may involve time and money spent for family visits and reunions. Whatever it takes, be family—*and* friends—with your family.

The Golden Rule Begins at Home

Homebuilding is not about floor plans, paint, wallpaper, and the number of bedrooms you have. It's about overseeing the relationships right under your home's roof. How would you describe the atmosphere in your home? For instance, what do you hear? Bickering? Yelling? Arguing? Angry words? Whining? Complaining? Tattling? Back talk? If any of these "sounds" describe the scene where you live, you have some serious homebuilding to do. None of these sounds indicate a Spirit-filled home where God's standards are supposed to be lived out. According to the Bible, every one of these expressions of emotion is sin.

The solution? Jesus tells us to live by the Golden Rule. He described it in two different verses: "Whatever you want men to do to you, do also to them" (Matthew 7:12). And, "As you want men to do to you, you also do to them likewise" (Luke 6:31). Simply put, do to others what you would want them to do to you. Treat others as you would like them to treat you.

Living the golden rule at home starts with you, mom. I truly believe and try to live by the truth that "who you are at home is who you really are." That's why modeling is such a powerful force in shaping how your daughter grows up. If she sees you being angry and irritated, and hears you yelling and screaming at her and her siblings, and even at Dad, she is learning—from *you!*—that this behavior is okay. And the opposite is just as strong. If she experiences firsthand your love, and sees you being tender, kind, and compassionate, and drinks in your sweet speech and wise words...well, message delivered! So...

First, live the golden rule. Check your own heart and actions. What's coming out of your mouth? Are God's tender mercies on display in the way you treat your children and husband—and even the dog?

Second, set some rules. With your husband, determine what behaviors are in and out. For starters, loud outbursts, verbal abuse, put-downs, name-calling, and hurtful physical contact are out. You will also need to plan ahead and determine the consequences of breaking the few rules you set. The goal is family love.

Third, enforce the rules. Unfortunately, being the homebuilder means you have to also be the enforcer. Follow your plan to uphold the few rules you set, and follow through on the consequences. Hang in there. If you do, your daughter and her brothers and sisters will get the message!

Fourth, focus on the importance of family. It's hard for a young person to realize that family is more important than friends. Friends come and go, but family is forever. Train your daughter from Day #1 to be the best sister she can be—sweet, helpful, kind, and encouraging.

Reaping the Blessings

God promises blessings to those who honor one another. And your family life can be one of His richest benefits. Home is where the people are who matter the most to you, and they should matter the most to your daughter as well. And yes, her brothers and sisters are probably noisy, nosy, and nuisances. And yes, you and her dad aren't perfect parents. But as you do your work as the homebuilder, your daughter will know beyond a doubt that you are trying to be a mom after God's own heart, a mom who is passionately committed to raising a daughter after His own heart.

You Can Do It!

Each of the following suggestions is something you can do to contribute toward becoming the mom you dream of being. And each one betters your life...and your daughter's too. Here we go:

Help your daughter learn to pray for her family.

Prayer is your answer to so many of the issues, concerns, and seasons you will go through with your daughter. So teach her this same practice. And teach her to pray for her family. Your daughter can't help but feel like she's a part of her family as she prays for each brother, sister, her dad, and even you. Imagine how her faith—and her love—will be strengthened as she invests her time and heart in praying for her family.

Involve your daughter in the family.

Unfortunately, most kids complain about their families, and your daughter can pick this up and begin to feel the same way. She decides that her family and being with them is a drag, that real life and fun is any place where her family isn't. So she begins to contrive to be out of the house as much as possible, or she just stays in her room. This is your cue to go into action! You, as the watchwoman, the shepherd, the steward, the mom, and the homebuilder must make sure she stays connected to family. Solution? Give her projects to do that benefit the family. She can help set the table for everyone. She can bake cookies for the family and serve heaping platefuls to her brothers and sisters. She can take a survey of where each family member would like to go on the next family vacation. Let her keep the family calendar so she knows what's coming up in each person's schedule. Curb her selfishness by showing her how to care about family and especially how to love them.

Involve your daughter in caring for the family.

Love for others is lived out—and grown—as we serve and care for others. Part of training your daughter (and all your children) is to involve her in serving her family. And yes, that includes big and little brothers and sisters! And yes, it includes doing her chores, just like her siblings. But remember, she's a little woman after God's own heart in training. You are grooming her for the future. Wherever she ends up and whatever she does, she will always have a place to take care of and people to serve. Allowing her to be a passive member of the family where you, mom, do all the serving creates a selfish—and handicapped—daughter. Please don't let this happen. Show her how to love her family. Include her in your efforts to serve and love one another beginning right under her own roof with her very own family.

Involve your daughter in the extended family.

And don't forget grandparents, aunts and uncles, and cousins! Include your daughter as you stay in touch with both sides of the extended family. Let her draw a picture or doodle, or add a sentence to any notes or e-mails you write to family. Encourage her to send her school picture to long-distance family members. Are you purchasing a birthday gift for some kin? Let her go with you and help select and even gift wrap it. Planning a family gathering? Ask her what she thinks everyone would like to eat and do. Maybe you could even enlist her help in making some party favors or a photo album! And here's a fun project: Spend time together researching her family heritage. Who knows? Maybe she'll discover she's a distant descendant of Davy Crockett, like I am!

Make your home the place to be.

As a parent, there are so many things you must train your daughter to do, and this will require that you insist on her participation. That's because they are important for helping her to develop a sense of "family." But along the way, you can have fun and make your home the place where your daughter wants to be (as well as her friends). As you invest in and nurture your own daughter, she will sense your love and sincere interest. She will want to be with you. And because you are such a neat mom, she will want her friends to be around you! Isn't that the way you want it? Instead of having your daughter go to a friend's house where the parents might be absent or disinterested, make your home the place to be, and welcome your daughter's friends—whether they be girls, tweens, or teens. Open your doors wide. Allow your daughter's friends to come into your home...and your heart. Let them come under your godly influence. Who knows? Her friends just might become girls after God's own heart too!

Mom's Think Pad

Before you move on to your next Mom Mission, take a minute or two to think about what you can do to track with God as a mom. Make some plans of your own to take a few small steps that can make a big difference.

1. I don't want to forget that my daughter sees and knows all. How she treats her family members will be taught—and caught—from me. So I need to look to myself first:

    Is there a family relationship I need to tend to?

    Do I need to be a better daughter to my parents?

    How am I doing in the in-law department?

2. I'm the one who is supposed to train my girl to "love one another." As I look at her attitudes and treatment of her dad, me, and any brothers and sisters, what behaviors and habits in her need my immediate attention...

    ...in the way she acts toward us as family?

    ...in the way she speaks to us as family?

    What is my big plan for making changes? For instructing my daughter in a better way? For laying out my expectations and enforcing them?

3. Oh yes—the golden rule! The way my daughter treats the members of our family is pretty much a reflection on me. Have I...

...been living out the golden rule myself?

...set clear family rules and guidelines?

...encouraged my daughter to be a cheerleader and helper to her siblings?

4. The Bible says, "The wise woman builds her house, but the foolish pulls it down with her hands" (Proverbs 14:1). In other words, a woman is either building her home and family in positive ways, or she's a one-woman demolition team! As a homebuilder...

...what destructive conduct and habits do I need to eliminate?

...what constructive conduct and practices do I need to take up?

5. Maybe we need a family motto, a family creed. Maybe I could start by sharing this one with my daughter and family: "Love each other with genuine affection, and take delight in honoring each other" (Romans 12:10 NLT). Hey, maybe my daughter and I could make a banner or plaque to put on the refrigerator door!

Chapter 9

The Cheerleader

*Encourage one another
and build up one another.*

1 THESSALONIANS 5:11 NASB

I grew up in the state of Oklahoma. One of this state's claims to fame is oil. In fact, there is still an active oil rig on the grounds of the state capitol, and to this day it is pumping black crude. Oklahoma is also the home to many of the descendants of the Five Civilized Tribes—that is, the five Native American nations: the Cherokee, Chicksaw, Choctaw, Creek, and Seminole.

And there is Football...with a capital F. During the fall, my growing-up town, like most others in Oklahoma, celebrates Fridays almost as if they were a holiday—maybe bigger than a holiday! That's because of Friday night football. I wasn't a cheerleader, but most of my girl friends and I were on the pep squad. When our team was winning, the crowd didn't need much to keep them going. But when our team was losing or it was a close game, the cheerleaders and those of us on the pep squad did our best to encourage both the team and the crowd.

Everyone Needs a Cheerleader

Why is it we typically think of cheerleaders and pep squads only in relation to sports teams? Everyone needs a cheerleader—even two or three—in their life to encourage them at all times, and especially when things aren't going so well. It's a fact of life that you and I—and our growing daughters!—crave encouragement from others, and others crave it from us.

Even the great apostle Paul needed encouragement. When he was under house arrest in Rome, he was concerned about his dear friends in the town of Philippi. So much so that he decided to send his trusted fellow-traveler, Timothy, to gather news about his friends so his heart and mind could be comforted and encouraged. He wrote to his friends, "I trust in the Lord Jesus to send Timothy to you shortly, that I also may be encouraged when I know your state" (Philippians 2:19).

I'm sure you've had your own bouts with discouragement and experiences that go something like this. You wake up to a beautiful bright new day, filled with all the hope and promise of joy, accomplishment, and fulfillment. And maybe things go well for at least a few minutes. But your first surprise comes way too early when you hear the trash truck making the rounds and realize no one put the garbage cans out the night before! And behold, this surprise is soon followed by a challenge—maybe a cross word from your husband that caught you off guard. Or a child who doesn't behave and you know you have to do something about it. Or (true story!) *before* you get your first cup of coffee, your espresso machine explodes!

And there are ongoing trials that can take us down. A child with a disability. A parent whose health is failing. A husband who's at home because he was laid off from his job. Maybe a teen who's rebelling on any and all points and simply will not listen to you and does not care. I'm sure you can add to this list of need-some-encouragement real-life situations.

Jesus Shows You the Ministry of Encouragement

What does it mean, as 1 Thessalonians 5:11 says, to "encourage" someone? I asked this question and hit the books to find out. That's where I learned that an encourager is someone who comes alongside another person. It's the same concept and word

Jesus used to describe the ministry of the Holy Spirit. When Jesus announced that He was leaving to return to heaven, the disciples were sorrowful, dismayed, and fearful (John 13:33–14:4). Jesus knew this and encouraged them. He cheered them on! He explained that He would send a Helper, another Person of the same kind as Jesus—the Third Person of the Trinity—who would take His place and continue the ministry of encouragement and exhortation that Jesus had to the disciples. He was speaking of the Holy Spirit (John 14:16), whom He would send to encourage us.

Then a few moments later, Jesus gave His disciples—and you and me—some final words of encouragement just before His crucifixion. Read on!

Jesus Gives You Encouragement

Times of disappointment, discouragement, and despair are a part of life—real daily life. I could give you endless examples from my life, the lives of women I know, and the lives of women, wives, moms, and girls who write to me and share their hearts with me at conferences. When I encounter one of these burdened and brokenhearted women, I often share one of my favorite verses. In it is the encouragement Jesus gave His disciples on His last night with them, the night of His betrayal, as they began to realize He was leaving them:

> These things I have spoken to you, that in Me you may have peace. In the world you will have tribulation; but be of good cheer, I have overcome the world (John 16:33).

Jesus knew you and I and our daughters, like His disciples, would be tempted to throw up our hands and give up when life becomes too unbearably demanding and difficult. Jesus knew this fact of life, acknowledged it, and offered encouragement, instructions, and hope. He did three things:

Jesus Told Us the Truth

Life will be difficult. "You *will* have tribulation." Jesus said this emphatically and clearly and factually. He communicated the black-and-white truth to us—the truth about trials and suffering,

Jesus Provided the Answer to Life's Tribulations

But Jesus wasn't done. On the heels of the bad news, He gave us good news to hang onto, beginning with the wonderfully hopeful little word *but*. By His own lips, He promised, "*But* be of good cheer, I have overcome the world." What is the answer to life's tribulations? It is Him! It is Jesus! It doesn't matter what you are facing—Jesus is your ever-ready, ever-present, ever-knowledgeable, ever-loving, ever-powerful source of encouragement. And Jesus prefaced His encouragement with this statement, yet another power-encourager: "These things I have spoken to you, that in Me you may have peace." The Prince of Peace gives us His peace.

Jesus Showed Us How to Encourage Others

Sometimes it's good not to say anything when someone is suffering. But eventually we must find the words to boost their hopes. That's what Jesus did. He said, "These things I have spoken to you." Jesus spoke words of encouragement. Words to point out truths from the Bible that comfort, that motivate and compel us and others to keep on keeping on. Words that inspire us in our desire to love and trust Christ and to live for Him—to be a woman after God's own heart—and to set a rock-solid example of strength and faith in the Lord for our daughters.

God's People Show You How to Be an Encourager

I'm sure you can recall how you felt when you were suffering or anxious or in pain. And then, praise be to God, some dear saint came alongside you and cheered you on with a smile, a hug, a tissue, a listening ear, a heart of love. And, in addition to all of these wonderful means of encouragement, this supersaint blessed you with the gift of words that lifted your spirits. Words that gave you hope and empowered you to go on, go on, go on. To keep trying. To not give up. To trust the Lord. Their ministry of encouragement ignited relief, courage, and energy in your heart.

For incredible lessons in Encouragement 101, the New Testament provides a roll call of godly people whose lives we can learn from. For examples par excellence, today's moms can learn from several giants of the faith in the Bible—people who understood and administered the powerful gift of encouragement to others. As you read, keep your daughter and her needs in mind. Ladies first!

Mary and Elizabeth

Mary, the soon-to-be mother of our Lord, had just been given astounding news by the angel Gabriel: She was going to conceive a baby by the Holy Spirit. Gabriel told Mary that her relative, Elizabeth, was also going to have a baby in her old age. Being pregnant and unmarried, Mary was in an extremely awkward and difficult situation. Probably only a young teen girl at the time, she made the decision to go visit Elizabeth.

To be sure, Mary's trip was definitely worth the arduous trek. The Bible reports that when Mary walked through the door of Elizabeth's home, immediately Elizabeth was filled with the Holy Spirit and greeted Mary with these encouraging, affirming words: "Why is this granted to me, that the mother of my Lord should come to me? For indeed, as soon as the voice of your greeting sounded in my ears, the babe leaped in my womb for joy. Blessed is she [Mary] who believed, for there will be a fulfillment of those things which were told her from the Lord" (Luke 1:43-45).

Christians, of all people, should be the most positive people on the planet.

After hearing these words of strong encouragement, Mary broke forth in praise and worship, and spoke her famous song or "Magnificat" that begins with these words of exultation: "My soul magnifies the Lord" (see verses 46-55).

Isn't it amazing what a little encouragement—a little cheerleading made up of a few words—can do to help a person accept reality, look forward to the future, and give praise, honor, and glory to God?

Barnabas

We first encounter several of Paul's traveling companions, including a man named Joseph, in the early chapters of Acts. Joseph was such a positive guy that the apostles in Jerusalem gave him the nickname *Barnabas,* which meant "Son of Encourage-ment" (Acts 4:36). We see the use of his nickname in full action when he arrived in Antioch on a mission. From the very first moment he stepped foot into town, his giving, ministering attitude is contagious: "When he came and had seen the grace of God, he was glad, and encouraged them all that with purpose of heart they should continue with the Lord" (Acts 11:23).

Paul

You would expect the great apostle Paul to be a cheerleader, wouldn't you? And that he was! For instance:

To the newly founded churches—"When [Paul and Barnabas] had preached the gospel to that city and made many disciples, they returned to Lystra, Iconium, and Antioch, strengthening the souls of the disciples, exhorting [and "encouraging"—NASB] them to continue in the faith" (Acts 14:21-22).

To Lydia—"[Paul and Silas] went out of the prison and entered the house of Lydia; and when they had seen the brethren, they encouraged them" (Acts 16:40).

To a region of believers—After "he had gone over that region and encouraged them with many words, he came to Greece" (Acts 20:2).

To his fellow shipmates—In the middle of a deadly storm in the Mediterranean Sea, Paul spoke these words of prophecy, truth, and hope to the passengers and crew: "Today is the fourteenth day you have waited and continued without food, and eaten nothing. Therefore I urge you to take nourishment, for this is for your sur-vival, since not a hair will fall from the head of any of you" (Acts 27:33-34). Then we are told that when Paul "had said these things, he took bread and gave thanks to God in the presence of them all; and when he had broken it he began to eat. Then they were all encouraged, and also took food themselves" (verses 35-36). Oh, and the outcome? With renewed hope, Paul's shipmates rose out of their despair and did what was needed to survive the storm. That very morning, they spotted land and were saved.

The ministry of encouragement is one that should be uppermost in your heart and mind. Christians, of all people, should be the most positive people on the planet. As a believer, you are indwelt with the Holy Spirit, the Helper. You possess "all things that pertain to life and godliness, through the knowledge of Him" (2 Peter 1:3). Therefore, since you have all these great spiritual blessings and resources—and more!—working in your behalf, "Be glad in the LORD and rejoice, you righteous; and shout for joy, all you upright in heart!" (Psalm 32:11). Share it! Shout it! Pass it on... starting with those closest to you at home, including your daughter, who needs daily encouragement.

Being Your Daughter's #1 Cheerleader

God never gives His moms an assignment without also giving them the grace and the means to carry it out. As I thought about the *how* of being your daughter's Number One cheerleader, my mind flew to the three-phase process God led me to put to work in my home and in my relationship with my girls. Here goes...and hang on. Once again, it begins with you and your heart, Mom.

Phase 1: A Decision

Like all women and moms, I've had my share of "one of those days." In fact, I've learned I should expect speed bumps, roadblocks, and ambushes in my days—maybe even a lot of them!

That's the message I discovered from the lips of Jesus when I read His declaration, "In the world you *will* have tribulation, pressure, affliction, suffering, trouble."[22] This knowledge was a wake-up call for me to get my head screwed on right every day, hopefully before the first surprise popped up all too soon.

So I made it a goal to seek encouragement first thing daily from God's Word. I wanted to be a positive woman and wife and mom. Every time I found a verse that brought me fresh confidence in God's plan, wisdom, and sovereignty regarding my days and my challenges—and my mothering—I marked it. I even coded these in the margins of my Bible so I could run to my Bible and find encouragement from God quickly when I needed it. (I also learned to keep my Bible on the kitchen table, open and ready for rapid and repeated access!)

Even to this day, when something is especially distressing in my life and a scripture lights up my day and floods the way with hope, I make a note of that breakthrough verse in the margin of my Bible. (Honestly, sometimes I think my Bible is more like my journal. Who needs a diary? It's all right there in my Bible!) After marking these "encouragers" for many years, all I can say is, who needs a pill or an "upper" when we can take in thousands of verses that deliver divine help to keep us moving forward with a positive outlook on whatever is happening? The Bible is the world's greatest miracle drug.

Now think about your daughter—your precious, beloved daughter. She needs you to be positive and a source of strength and support. The Old Testament King David asked the question, "From whence comes my help?" The answer? "My help comes from the Lord" (Psalm 121:1-2). The Lord's help is there for you, and it's there for your girl too. As He speaks to you each day right in your very own Bible, you are blessed by soaking up God's help and hope. And then you get to turn around and bless your daughter with it. You get to encourage her with God's strength and wisdom as she treks through the angst of her life. Be on your toes. Be alert. At the first hint of frustration or despair or disappointment, open your mouth and speak a word of encouragement.

Phase 2: A Deposit

Once I found God's treasure chest of words of encouragement, I memorized some personal favorites. I deposited them deep into my heart and mind. I wanted to be able to turn to them anytime, anywhere, as my personal on-the-spot encouragers and uplifters. I also highlighted them in blue in my Bible. What a wealth of spiritual energy, wisdom, and practical advice! Now whenever something happens or my thoughts turn down a negative lane, or fear rises up as I gaze at a problem or the future, I stop and turn to my arsenal of power truths.

And the same will be true for you. Once you store up God's gems of strength in your heart and head, you have power you can pass on to your girl. You can give her the wisdom of the ages. You can share God's personal take on each situation. At the first sign of discouragement in your daughter, or the first indicator of downheartedness (and mom always knows!), you have help to give—real help! This is a fantastic, natural way to teach truth to your daughter, to help her through hard times and show her how to turn to God and draw on His strength throughout life. And a big plus is that it's God's Word you are sharing, not man's. You, a mom after God's own heart, are depositing it into her young heart. Then it's always there for her to draw from when you're not with her.

Phase 3: A Divine Exhortation

One Sunday I heard a wonderful message on God's instructions to His people to be sure to "comfort each other and edify one another" (1 Thessalonians 5:11), or "encourage one another and build up one another" (NASB). The pastor explained that a part of encouraging others is *speaking* encouragement. It's sharing a "word in season" or "a word of encouragement." This can be done verbally, one-on-one or to a Bible study or prayer group, or at a mega-conference. Encouraging others can also be accomplished through writing—a book, a note, a letter, an e-mail, even a brief text message or Tweet! And its content is always aimed at giving hope to someone who's down or fainthearted. We are to "comfort the fainthearted" (verse 14) and "encourage the timid" (NIV).

After hearing this insight, I purposed to always seek to encourage everyone I talk to. I went a step further and put this goal on my daily prayer list. Going even further, I began asking God each day to help me remember to think of some truth from His Word to pass on to everyone I talk to, especially those who are hurting.

And guess who was at the top of my prayer list then—and is still at the top today? Guess who always gets (and should get) top billing for the first overflow of my ministry of encouragement? My family—my husband and two daughters! All those years ago I began, through regular prayer, to train myself in this new ministry. I actually began purposefully thinking about what my first words to family members would be each morning. Also, what would I share when they returned home from playing, from school, from work? Those words—which were powerful enough to set the sail for their day—had to be positive, affirming, uplifting, empowering, and hopefully memorable, something they could fall back on when the sea got tough. Heaven knows they would be getting knocked down and put down every day "out there" away from home...and for the rest of their lives! Isn't that what Jesus said? "In the world you will have tribulation." And aren't you glad Jesus added, "But be of good cheer, I have overcome the world" (John 16:33)?

Strength for Today, Hope for Tomorrow

Think about it. In one day at home or at school, there's a long list of possible failures for your daughter. For instance, a toddler falls down or pinches a finger or bites her tongue when she's trying to chew her food...or all of the above! Such a disaster equals howls and tears.

As a preschooler maybe your daughter isn't as fast at learning the alphabet or in running a race as someone else. The tendency is to drop out and stop trying, to withdraw and mope. Or maybe what's in her lunch isn't as "special" as what's in the other kids' lunches and she's the left-out one, the laughed-at one, or the made-fun-of one. Or maybe she was called on and didn't know the answer, or worse, gave the wrong answer! It's easy for a preschool-age girl to already think something's wrong with her.

And school-age girls? Well, this is when bad can go to worse! The trials and possibilities for failure only multiply. Kids can be cruel and mean. And bullies are for real. Girls start forming groups, and yours isn't a part of one...or the right one, or the best one. Schoolwork gets more difficult as the years advance. And keeping up with homework, exams, and papers becomes grueling. And we won't even talk about grades! And boys? Oh dear. "Handsome Popular Boy didn't speak to me or even look at me today!" Or

"Everyone's got a boyfriend but me! What's wrong with me?" Or, "Everyone else has a boyfriend. Why won't you let me date, Mom?" And there's always someone with more money, greater vacations, cooler clothes, and better grades. That's a given.

Into this deep pond of bitter water *you*—your growing girl's mom and her personal cheerleader—like Moses, get to cast in the elements that sweeten the waters that are poison (see Exodus 15:22-26). *That's* what the encouraging words you share with your daughter do for her! They heal her heart and make the everyday problems of life more bearable. God's words shared out of your heart become the one bright star in a black sky. Your words of wisdom and truth become the fuel that carries her to the end of a nightmare day. Just think: *You* get to give your daughter—whatever her age, and forever—the daily gift of loving encouragement and strength for her day and bright hope for all her tomorrows.

You Can Do It!

Each of the following suggestions is something you can do to contribute toward becoming the mom you dream of being. And each one betters your life...and your daughter's too. Here we go:

Encourage your daughter with your example.

Attitude is everything. And your attitude contributes powerfully to the well-being of your daughter. If your emotions swing like the pendulum on a clock, it won't be long before your erratic behavior has a negative effect on your daughter's emotions. What does the Bible say? "A merry heart makes a cheerful countenance, but by sorrow of the heart the spirit is broken" (Proverbs 15:13). Your positive and joyous attitude will be contagious—and encouraging. Remember, a cheerleader is most needed when things aren't going so well.

Encourage your daughter with your words.

When your little one is ill or your bigger girl is facing a big test, she needs encouragement. Or if your daughter's had a difficult day at school or when there's been a setback or problem with friends, your words can make a huge difference in your daughter's attitude and response. It's true that "anxiety in the heart of man causes depression, but a good word makes it glad" (Proverbs 12:25). There's enough pain and ugliness in the world, so choose "a good word" to offer to your daughter and make her heart glad. No daughter can ever hear enough praise, especially from the lips of her mom. So pour on the praise! As the watchwoman, put yourself on guard all day and watch for those times when you see your daughter doing something praiseworthy. Then make sure you let her know how wonderful she is! As another parent discovered, "Being a mom means praising your child. A lot."[23] And don't forget, whether you are putting your daughter down for a nap or bedtime or getting her up, or whether you are sending her off in the morning or receiving her back at the end of the day, do it with "a good word." She will carry your praise and assurance with her for years—maybe even for life.

Encourage your daughter with God's promises.

Does your daughter need a promise? The Bible offers us thousands of powerful promises. They provide a rich resource for you to share with your daughter from the moment she begins to talk. God's promises are there for the taking—like manna lying on the ground. They are offered to you, your daughter, and all believers by a faithful heavenly Father who does not promise anything He is unable or unwilling to give. Regarding God's promises, Solomon testified, "There has not failed one word of all His good promise" (1 Kings 8:56). Whatever your daughter is suffering—the painful booboo of a toddler, a fall from a bicycle as a six-year old, the trauma of getting her first C or D in sixth grade, or the loss of a best friend as a teen—God has a promise just for her. And you too! Here are a few gems you can share to cheer her on:

- ⌐ When she needs courage—Joshua 1:9

- ⌐ When she needs comfort—2 Corinthians 1:3-4

- ⌐ When she needs guidance—Proverbs 3:5-6

- ⌐ When she needs peace—John 16:33

- ⌐ When she need strength—Philippians 4:13

- ⌐ When she needs wisdom—James 1:5

- ⌐ When she needs a reminder of her worth—Matthew 10:29-31

Encourage your daughter with your prayers.

As you continually remind your daughter that you are constantly talking to God about her, she can't help but be encouraged. Your act of intercession demonstrates how much you care for her and desire her best as you bring her name before God. Your faith in prayer encourages her to have faith in prayer also. Copy the practice—and heart—of the apostle Paul. He consistently prayed for his young friend Timothy. In his letters to Timothy, Paul let his friend know that he was praying for him. He wrote, "Without ceasing I remember you in my prayers night and day" (2 Timothy 1:3). Why not cheer your daughter with these same words? Jot them on the napkin you put into her lunch bag. Put them on a note card you lay on her pillow. And don't forget to let her hear you pray just for her.

Encourage your daughter with the examples of others.

The Bible says we are surrounded by a "great cloud of witnesses" who have already "run with endurance the race" of the Christian life (Hebrews 12:1). You have already read about a number of examples mentioned in this book, including Jesus and Paul. From a tot in your arms to a teen who needs strong role models, you have these biblical examples to share with your daughter. So, from tot to teen, and beyond, a good mother-daughter practice is to read and study the lives and faith of the men and women in the Bible. (And don't forget to show her Miriam, Naaman's wife's maid, and Mary, the mother of Jesus, all young girls who exhibited great faith and courage.) And read through the stories of more modern-day examples whose lives exude encouragement. Fanny Crosby is a good place to start: She was blinded as an infant and overcame great adversity, writing thousands of our most beloved hymns, songs that encourage deeper trust in God. Let these examples cheer your daughter to "Go, girl, go!"

Encourage your daughter with hope in Christ.

What greater encouragement can your girl receive than the eternal hope offered in Christ? For those times that either you or your daughter are discouraged, Peter's words offer joy and hope: "Blessed be the God and Father of our Lord Jesus Christ, who according to His abundant mercy has begotten us again to *a living hope*" (1 Peter 1:3). If she is a believer in Christ, that hope is for today, tomorrow, and for all the tomorrows in her future. No matter what pain or trial your daughter will ever face in life, she can confront and endure them all with hope. Let Jesus cheer your daughter during those down times with these words: "Do not let your hearts be troubled. Trust in God; trust also in me" (John 14:1 NIV).

Mom's Think Pad

Before you move on to your next Mom Mission, take a minute or two to think about what you can do to track with God as a mom. Make some plans of your own to take a few small steps that can make a big difference.

1. Everyone needs a cheerleader…including me! I'm thinking now about how important encouragement was to me during my growing-up days, with all the challenges and emotions I faced. This serves as a good reminder of my daughter's need for a faithful cheerleader. In my own words, I would describe a cheerleader in this way:

2. Of course, Jesus is the all-time greatest encourager who ever lived. He spoke the truth and gave instructions for overcoming life's problems. What can I say to my girl the next time she's down or hurt?

3. The young Mary and her older cousin Elizabeth—I want that kind of relationship for my daughter and me! As I think about their time together, I notice that Elizabeth praised and affirmed Mary. Here's a list of five wonderful things about my daughter I can praise her for:

   —

   —

   —

—

—

"Lord, help me to follow through and cheer my daughter on by remembering to open my mouth and praise her for her many terrific qualities."

4. And Barnabas? I want to be a cheerleader, a "Daughter of Encouragement" to my daughter! Barnabas encouraged the people around him to continue on with the Lord with purpose of heart. What are some ways I can do the same for my princess?

—

—

—

—

"Lord, help me to remember to speak of You and point to You each time I talk with my daughter."

5. Paul, too! He really put his words to work—using them to strengthen and encourage others to trust in the Lord and continue in the faith. The verses that encourage me most—verses I could share with my daughter—are:

"Lord, sometimes it's hard for me to speak up, but please help me to open my mouth that I may share wondrous things out of Your Word."

Chapter 10

The Shepherd

I am the good shepherd.
The good shepherd lays down his life
for the sheep.

—JOHN 10:11

*I*t was one of those stories I knew I would never forget. In fact, 20 years later, it's still vividly imprinted on my mind's eye, especially every time I walk on a sun-drenched beach. I remember sitting in church on a Sunday morning. From there I was transported by the pastor's illustration to such a beach in the South Pacific. There, as the pastor explained, a bereaved husband had buried his wife in the sand of the shore of his new missionary outpost. He then set a solitary watch of one—himself—over his beloved's grave for several days and nights to ward off the heathen cannibals who were hovering in the thick palm groves just beyond the edge of the beach.

Later, when this missionary began his ministry and established contact with the islanders, several cannibals approached him with a question. They had watched him standing watch over his wife's grave and they wanted to know: "Who were those men with you on the shore?" They confessed that they had been ready to attack, but had kept their distance because the missionary was ringed by guards.

Just who *were* those men with him on the shore? Who knows? One can only wonder! But doesn't this scene remind you of the fact that "the angel of the LORD encamps all around those who fear Him, and delivers them" (Psalm 34:7)?

The Role of a Shepherd

Isn't God magnificent…and mysterious? Truly, "the secret things belong to the LORD" (Deuteronomy 29:29). We will never know on this side of heaven exactly how God surrounds and protects us. As happened with the missionary, "cannibals" of all kinds are lurking just behind the tree line of our lives, just out of sight. We can't see them, but we can know that God has encircled us with His love and protection.

Love and protection. Sounds like a mom to me! And also a shepherd—which is another aspect of being a mom who is aiming at raising a daughter after God's own heart. Just as the Lord is faithful to care for His own, a mom's mission is to keep watch over her child, her daughter. She is on assignment to ward off vultures, enemies, and cannibals who would harm her. Today's mom is not called to be hip, cool, and a barrel of laughs. She's called to be ever vigilant, to sleep with one eye and one ear open, to live her life as the shepherd of her sheep. In our case, that sheep is our one little ewe lamb, a precious, priceless daughter.

The Bible is filled with many illustrations that involve shepherds and sheep. These examples from the animal kingdom provide a good model of how a mom after God's own heart is to view her role as a shepherd. For instance:

- Sheep are dependent creatures who must be lead to food and water and protected from wild animals. Your daughter needs your guidance.

- Sheep cannot survive alone in the wild, but must always be in the company of a shepherd. Your daughter needs your presence.

- Sheep respond to the care and direction of the shepherd. Your daughter needs your love and leadership.

In Bible times, the Middle Eastern shepherd loved his sheep, gave each one a name, and cared for each one tenderly. And if any enemies showed up, the shepherd would place himself between his sheep and those wild beasts. Then after a long, busy day of leading and vigilance, he lay down and slept in the single doorway to his sheepfold. Why there? Because any enemy or predator would have to pass by him to attack his flock.

Burn this picture of the faithful shepherd into your heart, because this is how God's moms are to view their mission of being a watchful shepherdess over their growing daughters.

The Modern-day Shepherd-mom

Before we get to you, Mom, take a look at one of God's spiritual shepherds, the apostle Paul. Paul was instrumental in launching the church at Ephesus. You might say he gave birth to that church! For three years he shepherded that little Ephesian flock of believers who lived in the midst of a pagan society. After grooming a group of leaders, Paul moved on. But later, as he sailed home to Jerusalem, he landed on a nearby beach and called for the Ephesian elders to meet with him (see Acts 20:17-38).

What did the shepherd Paul say to the leaders of the Ephesian flock? He passionately appealed to them and pleaded with them as shepherds of that church to watch over and warn their flock for the sake of the people's spiritual safety and well-being. Paul's passion—and message—also applies to you as a mom with a daughter. Your girl needs your watch-care and wisdom for her security and survival. What are you as a modern-day shepherd-mom to do?

Feed Your Daughter the Bread of Life

It's no news to you that a shepherd makes sure the sheep have food. However, as your daughter's shepherd, "feeding" isn't necessarily speaking of providing delicious meals and snacks for her (which is always nice and welcomed!). It's referring to being her spiritual shepherd, to providing food for the soul that comes from God's Word, the Bible.

Look at Paul again. As a New Testament shepherd of God's people, he boldly stated, "I have not shunned to declare to you the whole counsel of God" (verse 27). For three years Paul faithfully taught God's Word to the Ephesian believers. No shortcuts were taken—he delivered the whole counsel of God. No food substitutes were used—he gave them the "pure milk" and the "meat" of the Word. No veiled messages were delivered—he clearly declared God's truth.

Jesus told Peter to "feed My sheep" (John 21:17), and in that verse, "feed" carries the idea of constant feeding and nourishment. This was a primary duty of a shepherd—to make sure his sheep fed on what was essential. And, in your case, your daughter deserves and requires substantial food. So, mom, as the shepherd, it is your joy and privilege to provide opportunities for her to feed on God's Word.

No, you aren't the sole provider of food, but you do get to make sure your girl is generously exposed to God's Word. You can find exciting and creative ways to...

∼ Encourage her at all ages to read and study her very own Bible. If your Bible is important to you, then it will be important to your daughter. Remember, a shepherd leads the way.

∼ See that she gets to church, Bible study, and youth group, where she will have opportunity to feed on God's Word. Remember, a shepherd makes sure to lead his sheep to the green pastures where food can be found.

∼ Help her make it a practice to have devotions, maybe even with you and hopefully with the whole family. Remember, a shepherd "makes" his sheep lie down and feed in green pastures (see Psalm 23:2).

∼ Bring God into daily life whenever you are with your daughter. Remember, a shepherd talks to his sheep.

Once you plan, prepare, and serve up God's Word with a cool, creative presentation (after all, presentation is everything), don't forget to pray. Ask God daily to work through His Word and His Spirit in your daughter's heart. Just be sure that you, as the shepherd, regularly and generously set the bread of life—the manna from heaven—in front of your gal so she can feed on it often and to her heart's content.

Watch over Your Daughter with a Vigilant Eye

A good shepherdess keeps a close eye on her sheep, ever watching for any signs that an enemy might be nearby. Paul spent three years shepherding his little band of baby believers. He was a faithful watchman. When he was leaving the Ephesian leaders to go back to Jerusalem, he acted like the shepherd he was and reminded them to watch over their spiritual condition and make it a top priority. He said, "Take heed to yourselves" (Acts 20:28). In other words, pay attention and be on guard!

And the same is true for you as a mom. Do everything you can to keep your head in the Bible. It will keep you sharp and alert. It will sync up your perspective with God's, and fine-tune your mom-radar for spotting enemies and wolves right away. (Yes, wolves love to prey on sheep!) So "be sober, be vigilant" (1 Peter 5:8). A shepherd watches.

As I am writing about the watching aspect of being the shepherd to my daughters, I can't help but remember a particular time when I had concerns about how things were going in their lives. I shared in another chapter that Proverbs 22:6—"Train up a child in the way he should go, and when he is old he will not depart from it"—became one of my "mothering verses." As a twentysomething mom, I rolled up my mothering sleeves and entered into the parenting process with full vigor! My mission? What else but to train my girls in the way they should go! I wanted them to follow God with all their hearts.

Well, about ten years later, when my daughters entered their teens, I, the watch-woman, noticed some attitudes and actions that bothered me. I shared my observations with my husband, Jim, and together we reached out for help from other parents who seemed to have their act together with their kids. Each parent was able to give some very simple advice, which was basically this: Set tighter boundaries, and restrict their friendships to those few girls and guys who would serve as a positive influence on their lives.

Believe me, watching—and doing something about what you are seeing—takes time! And attention. And every kind of energy—spiritual, mental, physical, and emotional. You will have to divert some of your time and energy away from the rest of your hectic life so you can focus on your daughter's heart and soul. A watcher is always on the lookout, always wondering: *What's going on in my girl's life? Who are her friends? Have there been any negative changes in her attitudes and moods? Are there signs of rebellion against me or her dad?* These are the kinds of questions you need to ask yourself as you watch over your daughter.

Warn Your Daughter of Danger

It's not enough to merely watch for signs that the enemy is approaching. The shepherd must also take the next step and sound the alarm—long, loud, clear, and again and again! The apostle Paul knew what the enemy was capable of doing and was very graphic in his description. Note the language he used:

> After my departure savage wolves will come in among you, not sparing the flock. Also from among yourselves men will rise up, speaking perverse things, to draw away the disciples after themselves (Acts 20:29-30).

Warning your daughter of possible pitfalls and impending danger is not always easy or welcomed. Your daughter lacks experience. And she has limited knowledge about the world and evil. Don't be surprised if she says something like, "Oh, Mom, why are you so uptight? Why can't you just let me have some fun? What's wrong with my friends?"

This is your cue to remember who you are: You are your daughter's mother and her shepherd, the one who watches out for and over her. No one loves and cares for her as much as you do.

And next, remember what it is you do: You watch and warn. Your role as a mother demands that you lead, speak up, and act. You are the parent who knows best. Whether it's popular with your daughter or not, you must do whatever it takes to protect her.

A wise mother knows that every age and stage of a daughter's development calls for different tactics and approaches. But here are some basic steps that will always guide you:

- ~ Begin your warning by reaffirming your love.

- ~ Review God's plan of salvation.

- ~ Share your reasons for being concerned.

- ~ Show her what the Bible says.

- ~ Keep on talking, regardless of her response.

- ~ Discuss the importance of the right kind of friends.

⁓ Let her hear you pray for her.

⁓ Don't give up, and don't give in.

Think about this comment made by a Bible scholar regarding Paul, the shepherd, and his willingness to faithfully warn his children in the faith in Acts 20.

> Paul...understood that there can be no growth in Christ without the transmission of truth. Are you fulfilling your God-given responsibility to declare God's truth to those he has sovereignly placed in your life—a spouse, a neighbor, a child? Or are you hesitating and shrinking back from such a task? The only way to have a clear conscience is to trust God and boldly speak out.[24]

The rewards for your perseverance in shepherding your daughter God's way will be great, not only now but for a lifetime to come, and beyond.

Living Out Your Shepherding Role

Neither one of our daughters dated much, for which we are eternally grateful. But there were, as with all girls, times when they thought they had crushes on what we knew were the wrong guys. What were the flashing signals that alerted us? Both Jim and I were uncomfortable with the lack of spiritual maturity in these young men. Some had obvious character issues that we, the watchers, noticed and didn't like at all! So we learned to go to the mat with our daughters and speak up. We put our foot down, so to speak. And we did what our advisors suggested and brought in the boundaries and restricted our daughters' friendships with these guys. It wasn't easy, it wasn't fun, and it wasn't pretty. And sometimes there was weeping and wailing. But we did what had to be done. And a bonus? Both of our daughters—and their husbands—have thanked us for our protective efforts, for being faithful shepherds.

I don't know what stage of parenting you are in right now, but don't lose heart. Lean on the Lord and hang in there. The rewards for your perseverance in shepherding your daughter God's way will be great, not only now but for a lifetime to come, and beyond. And be encouraged! Others have gone before you and have and are also facing your same concerns. Do what I did and don't hesitate to seek advice from others. Don't be too proud to ask for help. Remember, every parent's been there. You may discover that your situation is not as serious as you think, or as difficult to fix as you've assumed. Plus the reassurance of others will strengthen you for even larger battlegrounds as your daughter matures.

Entrusting Your Daughter to God

And now for some good news—the ultimate good news! You have God on your side. He's there, He's available, and He's totally capable. Therefore you can entrust your daughter into His hands. This doesn't eliminate what you, her parent, must do. You still have to live out your part in raising your daughter to follow God's heart. You still have to resist the pressure society puts on you and your daughter. But once you have watched and warned, and fed and led your little sheep, you can commit her into God's keeping. Then comes prayer and more prayer!

Trust in Prayer

When Paul told the Ephesian leaders, "I commend you to God" (Acts 20:32), he was demonstrating his commitment to trusting God and praying for those he had poured his life into—His sheep. In fact, he spent his life praying not only for the Christians he knew, but for believers in all the churches![25]

Well, dear mom, your daughter is definitely your sheep, a sheep you do a lot of things for. You have spent your life focused on that little girl from the moment you received the news that she was on the way. You decorated a room for her. You made sure you lived in the best neighborhood possible for her sake. You have searched for the best schools for her education. You have made sure she is well-rounded by letting her engage in piano lessons, gymnastics, soccer, swim lessons, camp, and, of course, a good home life. You have loved her, raised her, fed her, protected her, and trained her. But in the final analysis, your physical and financial attention cannot achieve the spiritual results that are available to her when you pray for her. Why?

Because without prayer, your natural parenting has little or no supernatural influence. Because prayer indicates your dependence on God. Because prayer is one way to ask God how to raise a daughter after His own heart. Your human efforts might raise a daughter who will be an okay person. But prayer contributes to your raising an exceptional person—a daughter after God's own heart. Isn't it reassuring to know that through all the days and nights of raising your daughter you can trust God to hear and answer your prayers for her?

So when it comes to your daughter, trust in God, and trust in prayer. And...

Trust in God's Word

The apostle Paul commended his Ephesian friends to "the Word of His grace, which is able to build you up" (Acts 20:32). He set the Ephesians before God in prayer, and then set the Bible before the Ephesians. So, like Paul, pray! And, like Paul, see yourself as the shepherd who makes sure his sheep have substantial food. Set God's Word in front of your daughter from age 0 to 20 and up! Trust God to use the Scriptures for her spiritual growth and maturity. Yes, savage wolves will come to hover around your girl. But a knowledge of God's Word will help keep her wise and safe. She will have the resources to guard herself against harm and evil.

Trust in the Lord

Here's a sweet benediction packed with promises for you as you parent your daughter and raise her to love God. I've motherized it just for you!

> Blessed is the mom who trusts in the LORD,
> and whose hope is the LORD.
> For she shall be like a tree planted by the waters,
> which spreads out its roots by the river,
> and will not fear when heat comes;
> but its leaf will be green,
> and will not be anxious in the year of drought,
> nor will cease from yielding fruit (Jeremiah 17:7-8).

You Can Do It!

Each of the following suggestions is something you can do to contribute toward becoming the mom you dream of being. And each one betters your life...and your daughter's too. Here we go:

Provide care for your daughter.

Psalm 23:1—"The LORD is my shepherd; I shall not want." Because the Lord is your shepherd, you can know that you will never have a need that God doesn't take care of. You will never lack anything. The Good Shepherd takes care of and provides for His children. Your mission? To be a shepherd to your daughter. To provide everything she needs—not wants. From Day One, food and clothing are givens on her Need List. Your time and love are needed. Your teaching and instruction are vital and help safeguard her each day and into her future. And safety and health are under your watch-care as well.

Provide rest and peace for your daughter.

Psalm 23:2—"He makes me to lie down in green pastures; He leads me beside the still waters." Because the Lord is your Shepherd, He makes sure you get the rest you need and provides a place of peace. So, how's life under your roof at home? Are you making sure your daughter has the energy and health she needs to be a girl who's growing up? Do you have a schedule for her rest? Set nap times and bedtimes? A specific time for lights out? A curfew? And, as much as relies on you, is your home a place of peace? You already know the world is filled with chaos. Give your daughter the gift of a place to relax and unwind, to read and pray, to think and discover her abilities. A haven. A sanctuary.

Provide healing and guidance for your daughter.

Psalm 23:3—"He restores my soul; He leads me in the paths of righteousness for His name's sake." A shepherd is always watching for the sheep that is cast down. Once a sheep is turned over, it will die if the shepherd doesn't come along and help it up. Then out comes the healing oil to rub on any wounds, followed by a time of closeness and affection with the shepherd. Likewise, the Good Shepherd...

~ Heals your spirit.

~ Restores you when you're cast down.

~ Retrieves and fetches you home when you wander.

~ Draws you back when you're unsure.

~ Relieves you when you're hurt.

~ Rescues you when you're in danger.

~ Finds you when you're lost.[26]

As the watcher and shepherd, you as a mom have this same wonderful ministry to your dear daughter. And guidance? Did you ever think you would be a guidance counselor? Well, that's you! As your daughter's shepherd, you not only walk the paths of righteousness she should walk, but from her first baby steps you point them out to her and encourage her to walk them with you.

Provide presence and comfort for your daughter.

Psalm 23:4—"Yea, though I walk through the valley of the shadow of death, I will fear no evil; for You are with me; Your rod and Your staff, they comfort me." From the cradle to the grave, loneliness is never a good thing. Your presence and availability to your girl are invaluable. Through good times and especially fearful times, you are there to tell her, "Everything's going to be all right. Don't worry. You have me *and* the Good Shepherd to see you through." Nothing could bring more comfort to a young heart in need.

Provide friendship and protection.

Psalm 23:5—"You prepare a table before me in the presence of my enemies; You anoint my head with oil; my cups runs over." The picture in this verse is of a traveler running from predators and enemies and finally arriving home, where all is well—complete with food, friendship, safety, and protection.

Doesn't this so describe a day in your daughter's life? Prepare for her homecoming each day, and welcome her home as a cherished friend.

Provide hope and home for your daughter.

Psalm 23:6—"Surely goodness and mercy shall follow me all the days of my life; and I will dwell in the house of the LORD forever." Where does hope come from? From the Lord. And from His promises. Never forget that every time you share God's Word with your daughter and encourage her in her devotional life, you are acquainting her with the Good Shepherd's promised goodness and mercy. Whenever your daughter is not physically with you, she can trust in the Lord. And home? Your shepherding mission isn't complete without providing a home for your daughter in your heart and in your house, a place where she is always welcome. And above all, continue to share the gospel of Jesus Christ with her so that she can, Lord willing, know that she has an eternal home with Him in heaven.

Mom's Think Pad

Before you move on to your next Mom Mission, take a minute or two to think about what you can do to track with God as a mom. Make some plans of your own to take a few small steps that can make a big difference.

1. Watching and warning. That's what a shepherd does for his sheep, and that's what I'm supposed to do as the shepherd of my daughter. What are some ways I can do a better job of…

    …watching over my daughter?

    …warning my daughter?

2. I realize how important it is to spend time in the Bible with my daughter. As I think about this, here are several daily opportunities I have for sharing God's Word with her that I'm missing out on:

   And here's what I plan to do about giving my girl the substantial food she needs from the Bible so that I, as a shepherd, am "feeding *my* sheep."

3. I really don't like to confront, and I'm not very good at it. And I *hate* being a nag! But, like Paul said, there are "savage wolves" and false teachers who want to destroy my daughter and undermine her faith in God. Here are some actions I can take in these important areas:

Pray for boldness to speak up the next time…

Plan how I will approach my daughter when…

Prepare which verses will help her with her problem of or with…

4. As I think about these verses that instruct me to watch over my growing daughter, I'm seeing some areas where I need to gear up!

Proverbs 27:23: "Be diligent to know the state of your flocks, and attend to your herds." How can I do a better job of this?

Proverbs 31:27: "She watches over the ways of her household, and does not eat the bread of idleness." Oops! Where am I failing here, and what will I do to pay closer attention to my daughter's welfare?

Chapter 11

The Marathon Runner

I press toward the goal for the prize
of the upward call of God in Christ Jesus.
—Philippians 3:14

As I look back a few years, I am shaking my head in disbelief. Was that really me who, at age 40, took up running? What was I thinking? And why?! Well, my husband Jim was committed to running, and I could see the many benefits he had gained from this single daily practice. So I decided, "Okay, one female runner, coming up!"

First on my "things to do before I start running" list was to drive over to the library and check out a pile of books on the basics of running. Then I dove in and researched proper clothing, running techniques, physical conditioning, and warm-up exercises.

After a time of knowledge-gathering and preparation (and I must say, shopping for one pretty cute outfit!), finally the day arrived when I actually stepped out of my house for my first-ever jog, thinking, *Ta-da! Here I am, world!* I closed and locked the door, took a swig from my giant water bottle…and made it all the way to the end of the block!

Well, it's a good thing that "a jog of a thousand miles begins with a single step." And, I want to add, *lots* of persistence. When I finally hung up my shoes, I was running eight miles a day and totaling 50 miles a week. During my running years, I never desired to run a marathon. But with my dedication and perseverance, I actually think I could have competed in, and maybe finished, the grueling 26 mile-385 yard Los Angeles Marathon.

Mothering Is a Marathon

Ask any mom, and she will tell you being a mother is the most challenging occupation of all. It's a 24/7 job that starts with a dream and continues forever. It never ends, never lets up, is ever-changing, and constantly requires your "A game," your best efforts, your unrelenting hard work. And then, surprise of surprises, in the very next breath, every mom will effervesce about the joys of motherhood and let the whole world know that nothing on earth compares to being a mom.

Mothering is like running a marathon, the world's most popular endurance race. It's not a sprint of a few hundred feet at maximum effort and then it's all over. No way! Raising a daughter after God's own heart is an endurance race—a race where you set the pace and the direction for you and your daughter. It's run day after day. And it's run for a lifetime. It is a race the two of you run together as you both "press toward the goal for the prize of the upward call of God in Christ Jesus" (Philippians 3:14).

How can you make sure you run the mothering race without giving in or giving up, especially during difficult and challenging times? Here are some tips on how to successfully run your marathon, the race in which you and your daughter are pursuing God's own heart.

Know Your Calling

Being a mother to that young lady of yours is the most noble of all callings. It's a calling from God, based on a stewardship of her life and training. And it's a calling affirmed by your unique bond and relationship with your daughter. You would think that every mother would consider this role as her Number One priority, wouldn't you?

I wish this was true! Back when I was an unbeliever, if you had asked me, "Are you a good mother?" I would have indignantly given an affirmative response, "Of course I'm a good mother. In fact, I'm a great mother!" Well, it took the transforming power of God's Spirit and some time in the Bible to discover that I was a miserably poor mother! Only as I grew in the knowledge of God's plan for moms did I begin to grasp that my first priority was to be a support and encourager to my husband and children. Since that day when I came to life in Christ, I have grown to know my calling—I am a Christian wife and mom—and what it is I'm supposed to do: I am to *love* my husband and *love* my children (Titus 2:4).

Once I understood these callings, I put my whole being into these two roles. As a mom of two little ones whose dad was gone for long stretches of time on missions work, or out many evenings as a teacher, or away while he was activated with the Army Reserves, I knew my calling: I was to keep the home fires burning. I was to keep on training and teaching our daughters. And, of course, I was to provide lots of creative fun times to help the time pass quickly!

Also, as our girls were closing in on marriage, my calling caused me to choose not to pursue writing until they were both married and our nest was empty. I thought, *Surely, it takes a* lot *of time to write a book,* time which I didn't think I had right then. Well, now I realize I had *no* idea how involved in writing books I would be! I'm so thankful that I waited until the girls were off starting up their marriages. It was the right decision for me at that time.

Know What It Is You Do

It has now been 30-plus years since I embraced God's role for my life. And I have to say, that role has never budged, changed, or shifted. Yes, the nest has been empty for some time, but as I am writing to you, guess what? I'm still a mom! That will never change for me, and it won't for you either.

So I want to encourage you to carve out some time (which I know won't be easy!), and sit in a quiet place (if you can find one!) and think through your purpose, especially as it relates to being a mom. Once you get your role as a mom fixed in your heart and mind as a top priority, you'll see things change. Once you embrace what it is you are to do, you will bound out of bed every morning with all of the confidence, direction, and purpose in the world. Why? Because you know your focus for that day, and all the days of your life. You know what it is you are to do, today and every day—you are a mom.

Know Your Goal

Jesus made a statement about the impossibility of serving both

God and money, and I believe the principle applies to you and me as moms. He said, "No one can serve two masters; for either he will hate the one and love the other, or else he will be loyal to the one and despise the other" (Matthew 6:24). Jesus is saying that you and I cannot serve two masters equally. His remarks are aimed at exposing divided loyalties. Here's how this principle worked in my life.

I had two little girls, ages one and two...but I also had a desire for an advanced educational degree. So I enrolled in a local college and signed up for a full load of coursework. I found a babysitter and dropped my little toddlers off for daycare every weekday before daylight, and picked them up after dark. I was definitely serving one master (school) over another (being a mom).

Then when I became a Christian and comprehended who I was and what I was to do, I realized I needed to make a choice. Was I going to serve myself, or serve my new master, Jesus, which meant I was to serve my husband and children? So I dropped the master's program and began the real "Master's Program." You might say I began earning a master's degree in mothering!

My story is my story. And yours will probably differ in a number of ways. But ask God to help you settle in your mind and heart what it is you do and are to do. Open your heart to His leading. If you have children, you are a mom. That's settled and certain. And what you do should include being a mom after God's own heart. If you are a professional, a businesswoman, or a working mom of any kind, realize that, in God's economy, being a mom and raising a daughter after God's own heart is still your highest priority.

Know You Are Not Alone

Mothering is a solitary role. Your daughter has only one mother—you! No one else can naturally fill that role in your daughter's life, so no mom should take her mommy role lightly. And God has given you a multitude of resources to assist you in fulfilling your goal of raising a daughter after God's own heart. For instance...

God has given you His Word and His Spirit to help you run the race—Whatever the need, look to God for it. Do you need more love, joy, patience, gentleness, or self-control as a mom? These are aspects of God's "fruit of the Spirit" and they are available to you as you "walk in the Spirit" (Galatians 5:16,22-23).

Need more strength? Pick up your Bible and read any number of God's promises to you. Or, if you're on the run, simply recall a handful of the assurances you have memorized by heart.

Need more peace, or peace of mind? Just lift up your heart in prayer to the God of peace (Philippians 4:9) and enjoy His peace (another fruit of the Spirit).

Need some fellowship? If you are feeling like you're all alone in the parenting game, look up and look to God. He's right there, backing you up and living out His promise to "never leave you nor forsake you" (Hebrews 13:5). Let Him and His Word cheer you on as you cheer your daughter on!

Need friendship? Being a mom can get lonely, but in God you have "a friend who sticks closer than a brother" (Proverbs 18:24).

God is the One who tells moms to "love their children" (Titus 2:4), and He is the One who can help you do just that as you turn to Him, trust in Him, pray to Him, and rely on the truth of His Word.

God has given you older women for guidance—Look around! There are older women in your church who are a few steps ahead of you in the mothering race, and maybe even some who have finished the course. When you have a chance, read Titus 2:3-5 to get the full scope of the ministry these older women are to have in encouraging you as you run the marathon race of being a mom. That's their role. But God expects you to seek their help, and He's instructed them to give you help (verse 3). Ask one of these seasoned moms to meet with you, even if only for one time, so you can learn from her wisdom and experience.

This is exactly what I did during my girls' growing-up years. At each stage of development I would ask for advice from several moms who also had girls—and had survived those particular years of parenting. Like me, you can seek out a mentor. Allow one or more of these mentor-moms who are further down the path of the marathon ahead of you to help you master the demands of mothering. Oh, and don't forget! One day soon there will be some younger moms in your church who need *your* help raising kids after God's own heart. Then you can become one of the "teachers of good things" and encourage those "younger women...to love their children" (verses 3-4).

God has given you others who are in the same mommy boat—Many churches have groups of young mothers who meet together, such as Mothers of Preschoolers, or MOPS. Perhaps the women in these groups are in the same stage of life and parenting that you are. When they meet, it's not to pool their ignorance or to gossip. It is to share ideas, hear qualified and encouraging speakers, and receive instruction on how to lead their little ones through those early years. Rather than sail through uncharted waters alone, join with a fleet of moms. You are all sailing toward the same destination—raising a daughter after God's own heart. So enjoy the ride. Enjoy the camaraderie. Enjoy the sharing. And enjoy cheering each other on.

Know the Value of a Day

If you or I reflect for very long on what it takes to raise a daughter after God's own heart, we will probably become overwhelmed by the challenge. Think about it—here you are, a woman who's trying to make it through life. And God has handed you the stewardship of a human soul who will live for eternity. Yes, it's true that God is ultimately responsible for the eternal destiny of your daughter. But humanly speaking, you, and hopefully her dad, are responsible for her physical, mental, and spiritual development.

Before you throw up your hands in defeat as you ponder this long-term responsibility, consider the value of a day. A day consists of 24 hours. That's 1440 minutes, or 86,400 seconds. Every mother who ever lived was allotted the same measured day you now possess in your hands. Your job is to try your best to be the best mother to your daughter you can be—just for today. That's all God asks of you, and that's all God expects of you. Do your best...for this one day.

But your life is not over! God asks and expects the same thing from you tomorrow. So you wake up tomorrow, take what you've learned from your yesterdays—the victories, the defeats, any failures and slipups—and try again to be the best mom after God's own heart you can be for another day. There will be some goofs, crashes, train wrecks, and meltdowns. But the secret is to "press toward the goal for the prize" (Philippians 3:14) and not give up! The prize of a daughter who loves God is far too great to allow yourself to give in or give up when adversity or setback comes your way. But you do get the chance to make each day count. You do get to make the choice to live each day as if it is your last day with your daughter. If you only have today, what would you want to say to her? What would you want to do together? What would you want to make really sure she knew about you, your love, and about Jesus? What would you want her to remember about her last day with her mom—with you?

One day is all you have, dear mom. But eternity is wrapped up in it. So treasure today with your daughter.

Because each day is so vitally important, plan for each precious 24-hour span God gives you with your little, big, or in-between girl. Cherish it. Welcome it. Enjoy it. Make it count! Then evaluate it and adjust it so tomorrow is even better.

What will happen when you live out your parenting role one day at a time? For one thing, you will be giving your all. And you will be living it—really living it! And you will be relishing it. And, blessing upon blessing, you will be surprised to see yourself stringing good days together, one after the other. You'll revel in days when you think that things between you and your daughter couldn't get any better. Because you and she are having so much fun at this or that stage in her life, you will find yourself wanting to freeze each season of your relationship. (So be sure to take lots of pictures or audio clips. And record your joys in a journal. These good days are gifts from God!)

One day is all you have, dear mom. But eternity is wrapped up in it. So treasure today with your daughter. Don't let it just happen and slip by. One day, with God's help and grace, you will stand with satisfaction and amazement as you behold your beautiful-on-the-inside daughter, whose godly life is ready to brave society as a strong, vibrant Christian woman after God's own heart. A life that represents God's next generation. A life that is prepared to repeat the process she learned from you all over again in another home with her own little souls, if God wills. The psalmist penned it this way: "I will make Your name to be remembered in all generations; therefore the people shall praise You forever and ever" (Psalm 45:17).

Going the Distance

Do you remember what I shared about growing up in a football-crazy town and state in our chapter on the mom as cheerleader? For many of the people there, football was king! And as I close out this book on raising a daughter after God's own heart, I want to use the game of football to illustrate a few examples of moms who do or don't go the distance with their daughters. Keep in mind that a football field is 100 yards long—and a team cannot score a touchdown unless it reaches the *end* of the field.

The 50-yard mom—Many a mom drives up to the junior high school curb, opens the car door, drops her daughter off, waves good-bye, and says, "Well, I've taught you everything you need to know. Now go out there and do it!"

The 75-yard mom—This is the mom who hands her high school daughter the car keys (and sometimes even a car!) at age 16. She stands in the driveway, waves good-bye, and yells, "Well, you're on your own now. You can drive, you're old enough to get a job, and you know what you ought to do. Good luck!"

The 95-yard mom—This mom drops her still-moldable daughter off after high school graduation at a job or college and calls out to her, "Don't forget to visit us once in a while!"

The 100-yard mom—This is the marathon mom. She refuses to stop at the 95-yard line—or the 96-yard line, or even the 97-, 98-, or 99-yard line. Oh, no, not her! No way is she stopping. She signed on to go the distance, to make it all the way to the end of the field and across the goal line—to be able to say, "I have finished the race" (2 Timothy 4:7) of raising a daughter after God's own heart.

You can do it! You can be a marathon mom. God has already given you every resource you will ever need to run the race alongside your daughter. There is no reason to give up before seeing your daughter cross the finish line. There is no reason you cannot muster up the energy and effort and resolve it takes to accompany your daughter through life. Determine to run, to *really* run the mothering marathon. And, with every step, ask God to give you His strength, energy, and wisdom to see your mission to the end—that of raising a daughter who follows Jesus, a daughter who becomes a woman after God's own heart!

You Can Do It!

Each of the following suggestions is something you can do to contribute toward becoming the mom you dream of being. And each one betters your life...and your daughter's too. Here we go:

Evaluate your priorities.

It's so easy to think you are doing what's best for your daughter by making and spending money to provide your precious girl with things and stuff. And it starts early! From designer baby clothes and perfect baby decor to private schools and lessons, the latest fashions and phone, plus a television and the Internet in her room. Well, the list of perks is endless. But your daughter needs a mom who has mentally, physically, and spiritually placed her as a priority person right at the top of her list of VIPs along with her dad. She needs mom to help her with her heart and invest in showing her how to be a girl after God's own heart.

Work over your schedule.

It's easy to think your priorities are in order. But it's always good to double-check to be sure. Take a look at your calendar. And look again at the past few weeks in your daily planner. What do you see there about your commitments, your activities, your hobbies? Exactly where are you spending your time, and with whom? What is it that consumes the majority of your physical time and mental energy? What does this reveal about your focus? Who is receiving the bulk of your time and attention?

Make sure daughter-time shows up on each day, and daughter-dates appear once a week or so. To paraphrase and apply Jesus' words in Matthew 6:21, where the treasure of your time is, that's where your heart is too. Give your treasured daughter the treasure of your heart, your love, and your time. If you need to, turn things around. Start small. As you see results in your daughter and in your relationship with her, step it up and keep fine-tuning and increasing—and enjoying—your mommy efforts.

Start fresh each day.

Anyone who hopes to run a marathon trains day by day, and

day after day. That means a marathon mom cannot rest on yesterday's parenting results, good or bad. If they weren't so good, don't dwell on them...but do learn from them. And, if they were good, praise God. At the same time, don't rely on them or think you can slide a little today...but remember them. Start each day with a fresh, clean slate of desires, expectations, and dreams for your relationship with your daughter. And do the same for your role as a mom. What is it you can do to be the best mom you can be just for today? Name it, own it, and plan for it. And pray! Ignite your new day and your efforts with the power of prayer.

Make sure you are a hands-on mom.

Is your schedule keeping you from being more involved in your daughter's life? If so, ask God what choices you need to make that will give you more time with your daughter. Maybe you could start by getting up before she does, so her memories are not of you dragging yourself around like a zombie. (Most runners get up and run early—before the family even wakes up.) You'll be more upbeat, alive, and ready to give your sweet thing time and attention. Get dressed and ready for your day so you can help her get ready for her day and for school, if she's school age. Have breakfast together, or at least sit with a cup of coffee and chat with her about her day and her little life while she eats. If you work, try to take her and/or pick her up after school or be there when she gets home. If she's in school, be available to encourage her with her schoolwork, and help her with her Bible memory verses for church. Remember, your daughter thrives on your involvement in her life. Daughters naturally adore their moms and crave time with them, unless they are being pushed away or ignored. Then it won't take long for the wall to go up. The smart mom knows that *love* is spelled T-I-M-E. And the more, the better!

Demonstrate your love often.

All the little things that we've gone over in this book deal with showing your daughter you love and care for her. But it's always a good thing to verbalize your love. You can't say "I love you" and "I love every little thing about you" enough. And you can't demonstrate it enough. No child ever died from an overdose of love.

In fact, love demonstrated is what keeps a girl and her hopes and dreams alive.

Remember that raising your daughter is a marathon.

You are blessed with a built-in goal from God. You are to run the marathon of raising a daughter after God's own heart. What purpose! What a goal! And your run as a mom is no little short jog. No, yours is the granddaddy of them all, the long one—the marathon. The secret to running long distances is "hitting your stride." So when it comes to raising your daughter after God's own heart, find your stride, a rhythm that includes and excludes what helps and hinders your race. Try to settle into a pace of mothering that has as few variables as possible. Make your home—the place where your daughter lives—a happy, peaceful, positive place. Oh, and don't be surprised if her friends want to hang out there too!

Mom's Think Pad

1. Being a mom is a calling? And a marathon?! Hmmm. If God is "calling" me to "love my daughter" and raise her to love and follow Him, what do I need to change…

   …in my thinking?

   …in my priorities?

   …in the way I schedule my time?

2. I need to look at Jesus' words in Matthew 6:21 for myself. (Check here when this is done: _____.)

   Am I trying to serve two masters when God is asking me to focus on one goal—to raise a daughter after His heart? Here, Lord, are my first thoughts:

3. Thank goodness I'm not alone as a parent! I know this, but I don't always stop and remember that the Lord is near, and that He is my "refuge and strength, a very present help in trouble" (Psalm 46:1). To tap into God's power and wisdom, what do I need to do to…

   …get into my Bible for help with my problems?

   …spend some time—even a phone date—with an older woman for help with this mom thing?

...spend some time with other moms?

4. The value of a day—I've never thought much about this. My days just happen. I think I'm lucky if I make it through the day without losing my mind...or my temper! Right now it's _____ a.m./p.m. What can I do that's constructive with what's left of it?

And tomorrow? I'm going to start it with a plan to give it my all by making sure these three things happen...or don't happen:

—

—

—

5. What are the main excuses, attitudes, or bad habits that keep me from running in the marathon alongside my daughter?

—

—

—

"Lord, please help me to..." (complete your prayer for raising a daughter after God's own heart).

Notes

1. John C. Maxwell, *The Maxwell Leadership Bible* (Nashville: Thomas Nelson, 2002), p. 1217.

2. *Matthew Henry's Commentary on the Whole Bible* (Peabody, MA: Hendrickson Publishers, 1991), p. 244.

3. C.S. Lewis, as cited by Albert M Wells, Jr., ed., *Inspiring Quotations—Contemporary & Classical* (Nashville: Thomas Nelson, 1988), p. 119.

4. Harry H. Harrison Jr., *1001 Things It Means to Be a Mom* (Nashville: Thomas Nelson, 2008), p. 77.

5. See Psalms 77:12; 50:2; 40:10.

6. Tedd Tripp, *Shepherding a Child's Heart* (Wapwallopen, PA: Shepherd Press, 1995), p. 33.

7. Robert Moorehead, as cited in Wells, Jr, ed., *Inspiring Quotations,* p. 119.

8. *Life Application Bible* (Wheaton, IL: Tyndale House, 1988), p. 864.

9. William Law, as cited by Sherwood Eliot Wirt, *Topical Encyclopedia of Living Quotations* (Minneapolis: Bethany House, 1982), p. 182.

10. Wirt, *Topical Encyclopedia of Living Quotations,* p. 183.

11. Andrew Murray, as cited by Wells, Jr., *Inspiring Quotations,* p. 160.

12. Stanley High, *Billy Graham* (New York: McGraw Hill, 1956), p. 126.

13. High, *Billy Graham,* p. 28.

14. Elizabeth George, *God's Wisdom for Little Girls* (Eugene, OR: Harvest House, 2000), n.p.

15. Gleason L Archer, *Encyclopedia of Bible Difficulties* (Grand Rapids: Zondervan, 1982), p. 252.

16. Survey results, in George Barna, *Transforming Children into Spiritual Champions* (Ventura, CA: Regal Books, 2003), p. 41.

17. Mary Louise Kitsen, "Generations of Excuses," reprinted by permission.

18. Elizabeth George, *A Woman's High Calling* (Eugene, OR: Harvest House, 2011), p. 60.

19. See Genesis 2:18; Ephesians 5:22,33; Titus 2:4-5.

20. Adapted from Elizabeth George, *Cultivating a Life of Character—Judges/Ruth* (Eugene, OR: Harvest House, 2002), p. 134.

21. See Exodus 2:14-21; 3:2-10; 4:18.

22. Curtis Vaughan, gen. ed., *The Word—The Bible from 26 Translations* (Gulfport, MS: Mathis Publishers, 1991), p. 2108.

23. Harrison, Jr., *1001 Things It Means to Be a Mom*, p. 175.

24. Bruce B. Barton, ed., *Life Application Bible Commentary—Acts* (Wheaton, IL: Tyndale House, 1999), p. 349.

25. See Romans 1:9-10; Ephesians 1:15-16; Philippians 1:4; 1 Thessalonians 1:2-3; 2 Thessalonians 1:11; 2 Timothy 1:3; Philemon 4.

26. Adapted from Elizabeth George, *Quiet Confidence for a Woman's Heart* (Eugene, OR: Harvest House, 2009), p. 77.

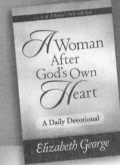

BIBLE STUDIES *for* BUSY WOMEN

Character Studies

Nurturing a Heart of Humility — MARY — Elizabeth George

Walking in God's Promises — SARAH — Elizabeth George

Old Testament Studies

Discovering the Treasures of a Godly Woman — PROVERBS 31 — Elizabeth George

Becoming a Woman of Beauty & Strength — ESTHER — Elizabeth George

Cultivating a Life of Character — JUDGES/RUTH — Elizabeth George

New Testament Studies

Living with Passion and Purpose — LUKE — Elizabeth George

Putting On a Gentle & Quiet Spirit — 1 PETER — Elizabeth George

Understanding Your Blessings in Christ — EPHESIANS — Elizabeth George

Experiencing God's Peace — PHILIPPIANS — Elizabeth George

Pursuing Godliness — 1 TIMOTHY — Elizabeth George

Growing in Wisdom & Faith — JAMES — Elizabeth George

Books by Elizabeth George

- Beautiful in God's Eyes
- Breaking the Worry Habit...Forever
- Finding God's Path Through Your Trials
- Following God with All Your Heart
- Life Management for Busy Women
- Loving God with All Your Mind
- A Mom After God's Own Heart
- Quiet Confidence for a Woman's Heart
- The Remarkable Women of the Bible
- Small Changes for a Better Life
- Walking with the Women of the Bible
- A Wife After God's Own Heart
- Windows into the Word of God
- A Woman After God's Own Heart®
- A Woman After God's Own Heart®
  Deluxe Edition
- A Woman After God's Own Heart®—
  A Daily Devotional
- A Woman After God's Own Heart®
  Collection
- A Woman After God's Own Heart®
  DVD and Workbook
- A Woman's Call to Prayer
- A Woman's High Calling
- A Woman's Walk with God
- A Woman Who Reflects the Heart
  of Jesus
- A Young Woman After God's
  Own Heart
- A Young Woman After God's
  Own Heart—A Devotional
- A Young Woman's Call to Prayer
- A Young Woman's Guide to Making
  Right Choices
- A Young Woman's Walk with God

Study Guides

- Beautiful in God's Eyes
  Growth & Study Guide
- Finding God's Path Through Your Trials
  Growth & Study Guide
- Following God with All Your Heart
  Growth & Study Guide
- Life Management for Busy Women
  Growth & Study Guide
- Loving God with All Your Mind
  Growth & Study Guide
- A Mom After God's Own Heart
  Growth & Study Guide
- The Remarkable Women of the Bible
  Growth & Study Guide
- Small Changes for a Better Life
  Growth & Study Guide
- A Wife After God's Own Heart
  Growth & Study Guide
- A Woman After God's Own Heart®
  Growth & Study Guide
- A Woman's Call to Prayer
  Growth & Study Guide
- A Woman's High Calling
  Growth & Study Guide
- A Woman's Walk with God
  Growth & Study Guide
- A Woman Who Reflects the Heart
  of Jesus Growth & Study Guide

Children's Books

- A Girl After God's Own Heart
- God's Wisdom for Little Girls
- A Little Girl After God's Own Heart

Books by Jim & Elizabeth George

- God Loves His Precious Children
- God's Wisdom for Little Boys
- A Little Boy After God's Own Heart

Books by Jim George

- 10 Minutes to Knowing the Men and
  Women of the Bible
- The Bare Bones Bible® Facts
- The Bare Bones Bible® Handbook
- The Bare Bones Bible® Handbook
  for Teens
- A Husband After God's Own Heart
- A Man After God's Own Heart
- The Man Who Makes a Difference
- The Remarkable Prayers of the Bible
- A Young Man After God's Own Heart

Elizabeth George...

is a bestselling author and speaker whose passion is to teach the Bible in a way that changes women's lives. She has more than 6.5 million books in print, including *A Woman After God's Own Heart* and *Remarkable Women of the Bible*.

For information about Elizabeth's books or speaking ministry, to sign up for her mailings, or to purchase Elizabeth's books, please contact her at:

www.ElizabethGeorge.com

or

1-800-542-4611

or

Elizabeth George
P.O. Box 2879
Belfair, WA 98528